the texas courthouse

first edition • gla press • copyright, 1971
by june rayfield welch and j. larry nance

Published by
G.L.A. Press
Dallas, Texas

Printed
by

Waco, Texas

Table Of Contents

Point of View· 1

A History of the Counties and the Courthouses· 4

The Courthouses· ·15

The Counties · 271

Bibliography· 332

Sources · 335

Index · 338

Point of View

To anyone growing up in North Texas before the Second World War the court-house was the capitol of all the world that mattered.

Of course, there was a Washington and an Austin and no question about the allegiance they merited. It was still a time when Texans stood at attention in a darkened theater as the flag came on the screen and the national anthem was played. No matter that it was four thirty in the afternoon and only ten people were present: two fat ladies in hats who rattled candy sacks and whispered so their words were audible throughout the theater, three little kids smelling of ripe tennis shoes and occupying the front row between trips to the water fountain, a high school couple in the far corner so lost in each other it was exciting and embarrassing at the same time to the boy and the pretty girl next to him who had had to pay a nickel of her own way in and whose hand he might summon the courage to hold if the movie lasted three months, and the pimple-chinned usher leaning against the back wall and pitching and catching his flashlight. With the first note of the Star Spangled Banner the popcorn was scotched between the chair back and the seat that flipped up and everyone was standing.

But nobody expected to see Washington unless another Boy Scout Jamboree was held there or one became a Rotarian or a Lion and went to a convention in Philadelphia or New York. Then one stopped by Washington because there would not be another chance to see Lindbergh's plane and the other Smithsonian stuff.

Washington was somewhere outside the actual world, a place read about in school and heard of on the radio, like Point Barrow, Alaska, and Hollywood and Van Buren, Arkansas.

Austin was also far away. It lay beyond mighty Dallas and fabled Fort Worth and seemed not to count for much in spite of a Texan's pride in San Jacinto and the Rangers and Jimmy Allred. The local legislator was a matchstick-chewing insurance salesman who ran his heels over and drove with his arm dangling out the window between waves. When the stock market crashed and half the county was out of work the state government was as helpless as everyone else. There would be a chance to see the great granite capitol with the star over the entrance on the way to the Alamo one day, but Austin was still beyond the limits of consequence.

Not so the courthouse. It was right there on the main street to be passed a couple of times a day if one lived in town or serve as a place to meet friends on Saturday if one did not. It occupied an entire block bounded by all the county's major thoroughfares.

There on the courthouse square old timers held interminable conversations consisting mainly of long silences, the inspection of passers-by, and trading knives. (John Graves' father-in-law had a great story about these friends of the courthouse. One friend arrived a little late one morning, found the benches filled, and hunkered in the courthouse shade next to an old colleague. They had long ago heard all of each other's stories. After an hour the friend said, "Well, how does it look to you?" There was a long delay and the colleague said, "I don't know. How does it look to you?" The friend chewed for awhile, moved back into the retreating shadow, and tested the earth with his pocket knife. Finally he said, "I think the sons of bitches are gaining on us.")

On a corner of the square stood the Confederate soldier, facing north (which one would deem interesting when he journeyed to the nation's capital and found the Confederate soldier in Alexandria, Virginia, with his back to the north). The soldier's narrow hatbrim and shoes, instead of boots, made him seem more pharmacist than defender of The Cause.

On the top floor of the courthouse was the jail. Prisoners were visible from time to time behind the bars and heavy screen fencing them off from the world. Sometimes they threw down money and asked kids to buy Bull Durham tobacco and OCB cigarette papers and whip licorice for them.

There at the courthouse was the best slide in the county, longer and higher than the one at the junior high school, and with grass to land in. More important, there was no danger of detention hall because "that is not an item of playground equipment but is intended solely as a means of emergency escape in the event of fire or other like catastrophe."

The big problem at the courthouse was the district clerk, an irritable man when sober and sensitive to noise on the fire escape landing outside his office. He had scattered any number of sliders who promised his retirement when they came of age.

The other hazard could be considered a blessing, depending on one's courage and competence. Sliders always brought breadwrappers to sit on, and the courthouse slide was incredibly slick from the waxed paper. Actually there was as much wax on the junior high slide, but heavy traffic had killed the grass and sliders landed on raw ground. The dirt they carried up on their trousers cut the breadwrappers' effectiveness. But with the courthouse's grassy landing only lack of nerve restrained the slider.

There at the courthouse officed the high sheriff and county attorney and other great men. There occurred trials that deprived men of liberty and sometimes life. And when a governor seeking re-election—or some upstart trying to unseat him—came to town, he spoke from the courthouse steps. During World War II scrap metal was piled high on the lawn as citizens donated material for bullets and battleships, and movie stars and hillbilly bands sold war bonds from a platform on the east side.

The clock measured off the hours and the bell sounded for those who could not see one of the four faces. There the ancient papers were kept. Legal notices two inches deep were tacked on huge pieces of beaverboard, and the dark halls smelled of homemade cigarettes and tobacco juice and creosote. The courthouse was the keeper of the credentials. There was the truest evidence of the ownership of land and brands. There were the records of birth and marriage and death.

But the most important feature of the courthouse was its form. The old ones suggested castles met long ago in tales of knights and kings and ladies fair. Between trips down the fire escape, sliders whispered of men imprisoned high above them, not those whose socks and undershirts were drying in the barred windows but others said to occupy the topmost reaches of the building, perhaps just below the clock or behind the gingerbread. Always someone present knew someone else whose uncle had a friend who once started home late from the Saturday night foot-and-onion show at the Lyric Theater and heard those poor wretches being flogged. It was usually the same uncle whose brother-in-law knew for a fact that periodically the city dropped a dead man into the standpipe to improve the quality of the water.

The age and grandeur of the courthouse, the roles it had filled, the dignity of its friends, and the stories they told—laced with ferocity and courage and wild humor—suggested a past rich in passion and perseverance and independence, so that one might believe something well worth knowing might be learned by a study of courthouses.

In early 1969, J. Larry Nance and I decided to visit all of the Texas courthouses. He would photograph each of them and I would write some of what we might discover about the counties and capitols. We set forth on the last Saturday in January, 1969, making the first of thirteen weekend trips to the 254 counties. We finished in April, having traveled some 16,000 miles.

Nance photographed all but two of the courthouses then. Those had been destroyed, Madisonville's by an arsonist and Crystal City's by county commissioners preparing for a new edifice. (About twelve of the buildings shown in Clark Coursey's *Courthouses of Texas*, published in 1962, were no longer standing seven years later.) Nance shot the old Lubbock courthouse the afternoon before it was demolished. The photograph of the Walker County capitol was made soon after another arson was done. (Weldon Hart, the master of courthouse lore, has a study group called BOTCH, Burning of Texas Courthouses, enumerating the capitols destroyed by fire.) Nance photographed the new Madison and Walker courthouses in 1971. The Crystal City shot was furnished by M. Dale Barker of the *Zavala County Sentinel*.

The book breaks down into three parts: a brief essay, the photographs of the courthouses, and finally notes on the counties. Studies are presently being made by experts in courthouse architecture, so no architectural comment was attempted here. Building costs were included whenever possible as reflections of the growth of the counties, their increasing affluence, and the declining value of the dollar.

County officials, chairmen of local historical committees, and others gave encouragement and invaluable assistance. We are beholden to them.

June Rayfield Welch
Dallas
July 1, 1971

A History of the Counties and Courthouses

Of some 3,049 counties in the nation, Texas has 254. They differ in size, population, wealth, climate, and other characteristics.

Some are big. Brewster County, with 6,208 square miles of territory, is larger than five Rhode Islands or three Delawares or a combination of Connecticut, Rhode Island, and the District of Columbia. Some are small. Rockwall County is only 147 square miles.

In population, Harris County has 1,700,000 residents; Lubbock County 170,000; Lavaca County, 17,000; Real County, 1,700; and Loving County, 170. (This set of figures was achieved by using only the first two digits of the 1970 census results in Harris, Lubbock, and Lavaca, knocking 100 residents off Real County and adding twenty in Loving County.)

Bowie County's average annual rainfall is 47 inches: El Paso County receives only 8 inches a year. Cameron County's annual mean temperature is 74° while that of Dallam County is 56°. Dallas County bank deposits total $5.2 billion, but neither Borden County nor McMullen County has a bank. Some counties grew out of Spanish departments and municipalities. Kenedy County was created in 1921, a hundred years after Spain lost Texas. But regardless of differences, the counties occupy positions of legal equality and their patterns of organization are substantially the same.

Alonso Alvarez de Piñeda landed at the mouth of the Rio Grande in 1519, establishing Spain's claim to Texas, but for the next century and a half local government remained only whatever forms the Indians used. Ysleta, established in 1682 by refugees from a New Mexico Indian revolt, was in Mexico until a change in the Rio Grande's course placed it in present El Paso County.

The establishment of Fort St. Louis by the Frenchman Réne Robert Cavelier, Sieur de la Salle, worried the Spaniards, although La Salle was killed and his colony failed. Having no colonists to move to Texas, Spain sought the allegiance of the existing Indian population, the Caddo confederacies, the strongest and most stable of the Texas tribes. They were situated in East Texas, on the edge of French territory. Missions were established to Christianize the Indians, teach them agriculture and trades, and make them responsible Spanish citizens.

The first Texas mission was founded in 1690. After a period of unconcern, Spain again established East Texas missions in 1714. Because the missions were so far from the entry point, San Juan Bautista, a rest and supply station was needed, and the mission San Antonio de Valero and presidio San Antonio de Bexar were established: in 1731 Canary Islanders founded Villa San Fernando, Texas' first civil settlement, near the mission and presidio.

At the time of Mexican independence, in 1821, San Fernando de Bexar (San Antonio) and La Bahía del Espirito Santo (Goliad) were municipalities. Nacogdoches was the only other settlement in Texas' interior. The Austin colonization efforts began in the last days of Spanish rule.

In 1824 Texas and Coahuila became a single state under the Mexican federal constitution. Texas was the Department of Bexar, administered by a political chief at San Fernando de Bexar. The departments of Nacogdoches and the Brazos were established in the early 1830's.

4

The departments were divided into municipalities which consisted of a town or towns and the surrounding territory. The governing body was the ayuntamiento, a council composed of the alcalde, regidores, the sindico procurador, the alguacil, and the escribando. In addition to presiding over the ayuntamiento, the alcalde had judicial functions. Regidores were councilmen. The sindico procurador was a prosecuting attorney. The alguacil served as a sheriff, and the escribando was the ayuntamiento secretary.

After independence the 23 municipalities became counties patterned after those in the southern United States. The county is an arm of the state although officers are elected locally and are not responsible to state officials. The county conducts elections, levies and collects taxes, maintains trial courts, and keeps order. For many years roadbuilding and maintenance so overshadowed other county responsibilities that members of the governing body were commonly called road commissioners. During the Republic all free males from age 18 to 45 and all slaves, 16 to 50, were subject to doing road work, an obligation that continued into the twentieth century in modified form.

Originally, the chief justice and justices of the peace together governed the county. In 1845 four commissioners replaced the justices of the peace on the governing body. Later the chief justice became the county judge.

The Republic's land area included half of present New Mexico and parts of other states, but the inhabited portion was quite small. Austin was established west of the frontier by President Mirabeau B. Lamar.

But the population was increasing. In 1836, it was some thirty-five thousand, excluding Indians. The 1846 census showed 102,961 whites, 38,753 slaves, and 295 Negro freedmen, a total of 142,009. In the first United States census, in 1850, 212,592 Texans were living in seventy-eight counties. Harrison County was the most populous, with 11,822 residents, followed by Cameron County's 8,541, and Rusk County's 8,148. The present big counties were: Harris 4,668; Dallas 2,743; Bexar 6,052; Tarrant 664; and Travis County, 138.

Altogether fifty counties were created in the 1830's. Bexar County's area was so large that 128 counties were created from it. There was effective resistance to the proliferation of counties during the Republic, but soon after statehood 31 were created at once. Sixty-six more were added in the fifties, placing all territory east of the 100th meridian within a county. The frontier receded before the Indians during the Civil War, so that only six counties were created in the 1860's. Sixty-nine came into being in the seventies, mostly because the Comanches had retired to the reservation. Sixteen counties were formed in the eighties, five in the nineties, two in the 1900's, and eight from 1910 to 1919. Kenedy County, the 254th, was added in 1921.

The Texan believed in self government and wanted a courthouse as near as possible. As population increased new counties were made from parts of existing ones. Counties were provided as the frontier moved westward. Once created, several considerations favored early organization. First, a county was administered by another until it was organized. There was predictable resistance to the idea of subordination, taxes assessed by the supervising county smacked of taxation without representation, and settlers resented traveling to another county to handle legal business. Most of all, lack of organization evidenced rawness and retarded development, since many prospective settlers preferred to wait until an area was somewhat civilized.

Growth was important and rapid growth desirable. An expanding population meant increasing property values and a diminution of the loneliness of the frontier, less incidence of the depressions that beset the pioneer. A character in Allen LeMay's fine novel, *The Searchers*, says, "This is a rough country. It's a country knows how to scorn a human man right off the face of itself. A Texan is nothing but a human man way out on a limb. This year, and next year, and maybe for a hundred more. But I don't think it'll be forever. Someday this country will be a fine good place to be." The sooner Texans augmented their numbers the better their odds would be against the land, the elements, and the Indians.

The early Texans were movers or builders. The mover went beyond the settlements to hang onto a precarious existence until civilization almost caught up with him. Then he would sell his improvements and begin again farther west. The builder took up a place where his dreams would finally come true. He became a booster in the fashion of the settler who said, "West Texas is so healthy that if a man wants to die he will have to go somewhere else to do it." Tascosa *Pioneer* editor C. R. Rudolph wrote that Austin would never approach the size Tascosa would attain. With the railroad in prospect he proclaimed, "Great is Tascosa. Great is the Panhandle. Great is the Denver, Texas and Fort Worth, livest and best paying road of its time." Rudolph, on learning that the XIT Ranch intended to run a telephone line into town, said, "Verily, there are friends and circumstances at work for thee, Tascosa, and thy days are to be long in the land and full of honors." Sometimes builders became movers when events destroyed their hopes, as when fences and the rise of Amarillo killed Tascosa.

County making was divided into two stages. Once created, a county had to have a certain number of residents before it could organize. Counties sometimes resorted to subterfuge to become independent. In 1890 Castro County had only 9 citizens and was attached to Oldham County for supervision. Organization required a petition reflecting 150 residents. After everyone in the county was listed in 1891 there were not nearly enough signatures. Strangers passing through signed, and the names of residents' relatives who had never seen Texas were affixed. Finally James Carter, of the Seven Up Ranch, gave his horses last names and signed for those Carters. The Oldham commissioners approved Castro's organization late that year.

The 1845 constitution, guarding against excessive county making, forbade creation of a new county that would reduce an existing one to an area of less than 900 square miles. A county was to be of such size—and the courthouse was to be so centrally located—that every citizen might be able to travel to the county seat, vote, and return home within a day. A 30 mile square would permit that degree of accessibility. In 1876 Armstrong County and 53 others were formed from Bexar by a "paper survey," a process the *Armstrong County History* describes as, "laying a ruler on a map and drawing lines 30 miles apart each direction." The technique disregarded terrain so that Wayside was separated from Claude, the county seat, by Palo Duro Canyon.

Usually the seat of government was to be within five miles of the center of the county, a requirement that made necessary an early survey. The first instrument in the Cooke County deed records is the bond and oath of the surveyor Daniel Montague, who swore, among other things, that he had "not fought

6

a duel with deadly weapons . . . nor sent a challenge to fight a duel with deadly weapons nor have I acted as a second . . ."

The location of the county seat was a matter of much importance. Prospective capitals might be towns or only unimproved sites, and partisans employed every kind of persuasion in county seat elections. Cooke County Chief Justice Robert Wheelock used a jug of whiskey to encourage selection of the Gainesville site.

Usually the owner donated the townsite, the increased value of the remainder of his land more than compensating him for the gift. After setting aside a courthouse square the county sold lots. The proceeds were used to cover early expenses such as building a jail and housing county offices.

In establishing the new town some early tasks had to be undertaken. A public well or cistern would be needed on the square. A watering trough would have to be built. The commissioners appointed to locate the Rusk County capital permitted residents of the new town of Henderson "to cut the timber out of the two main streets, fifteen feet each way from the center of the street, and to cut all the timber in the alleys by cutting the stumps even with the ground . . ." Before the Grayson County courthouse was built a pecan tree accomodated in its shade Sunday preaching and court on other days. The tree served as bank and post office. By general assent valuables left there were not to be touched. An old coat hanging from a limb took care of postal business. One going on a trip would sort through the letters in its pockets and take those addressed to points along his route.

Other towns did not always consider the matter closed after a county seat designation was made. Sometimes struggles over the location of government lasted for years, with removal elections called as often as the statutes permitted. Springfield had long been the Limestone County seat when Groesbeck began its efforts to become the capital. The Houston and Texas Central Railroad did not build to Springfield, and after an 1873 courthouse fire Groesbeck won a removal election. Later considerable dissatisfaction was caused by the inferior construction of the Groesbeck jail and courthouse and there was substantial sentiment for moving the county government. In an 1888 election, Mexia received 1726 votes to Groesbeck's 1130, but Groesbeck retained the courthouse since a 2/3 vote was required.

Sometimes it was necessary to do more than just win an election. Oil activity caused Monahans to outgrow Barstow, and Ward County citizens, twice in a six month period, voted to make Monahans the county seat. On June 14, 1938, moving vans appeared, unannounced, in Barstow. Monahans volunteers helped movers load county records, while a deputy county clerk sped to Kermit for a restraining order to keep the government at Barstow. The order was ineffective, and county officers were housed at the Monahans city hall until a courthouse could be built.

The creation of a county from another made it necessary that copies be made of the old county's records pertaining to land in the new jurisdiction. Morris County's was the usual solution. When it was created in 1875, two men were hired at 4¢ per 100 words to go to Titus County and transcribe the old records.

Having been organized, a capital chosen and officers elected, the county was ready for business. On May 11, 1885, Reeves County commissioners ordered the sheriff to buy a water bucket, a dipper, and a broom for their use. They paid $5 for an inquest on a man who died at Toyah but denied a $60 medical bill. The Pecos *Enterprise* decided the commissioners "figured if the doctor couldn't save the man's life he was entitled to no pay."

7

Actually the Reeves County commissioners first met on January 12 and rented a back room for county use. There was no quorum at the February 9 meeting: when the same thing happened February 19, Judge R. L. Horrell ordered the sheriff to bring in County Commissioner Ruben Richards. Evidently Richards' feelings were hurt, because he voted against everything that came up and then resigned.

Typically a county's courthouse history began with borrowed or rented quarters, the county clerk's front room or a corner of the hotel lobby. The earliest sessions of the Jefferson County Court were held above Beaumont's Millard and Pulsifer Store. Because some Texans had developed the habit of burning down the courthouse to get rid of indictments against them, sometimes owners of rented quarters required the clerks to take the records home each night.

The first courthouse was a rude affair, a log cabin if the country was timbered. Gainesville's $29 log courthouse had a dirt floor and no chimney. Early settler W. R. Strong said of it, "once in fly time, Uncle Jim Dickson's old steer went inside for shelter and when he tried to get out, he ran into one corner of it and tore it down." The 1847 Grayson County courthouse was dismantled in 1858 as a result of a wager on whether a goose was nesting under the floor. The sheriff had to dig the door out from under the wreckage to post legal notices required by law to be displayed on the courthouse door.

In neighboring Fannin County, the 1839 courthouse at Old Warren was, "of post oak and cedar log body 18 by 24 feet, one and one-half stories high, and a lower floor of rough plank, the upper floor to be dressed, and a wooden chimney, two floors and four windows (twelve lights) with shutters; one flight of stairs, the upper apartment to be divided into two rooms of equal size and one alley; to be covered with good oak boards three feet long, nailed to good rafters with one foot to the weather; to have a shed room at the opposite end from the chimney fifteen feet wide, which is to be of the same material and covered in the same manner as the body of the building; to have a good rough floor; with a door and window in each end of it and that each end of said shed room to have a small sufficient room for Commissioners Court, a bar ten feet long and four benches with back eight feet long, a clerk's table, with a large drawer and lock and key."

With its second capitol the county advanced from a log cabin—or a dugout on the High Plains—to an edifice of sawed planks such as the 1853 Hunt County building. Being the seat of government placed a town above other county communities. That distinction was symbolized by the courthouse. But the county seat town was also part of a larger society: it was important that the courthouse compare favorably with those of other counties. By the time the third building was needed the county was completely settled and sufficiently affluent to keep up with the courthouse Joneses. It would embody the glory of the county.

Thus began, in the last decades of the 19th century, the golden age of the Texas courthouse. The architect's task was to design a dignified building reminiscent of the grand structures Texans had seen elsewhere or read about or imagined. Ellis County's capitol is said to be in direct line of descent from the Allegheny County, Pennsylvania, seat at Pittsburgh. Irish architect J. J. E. Gibson built at Center a castle such as he remembered in Ireland.

Perhaps because Texans lived in plain houses and had little dramatic scenery, they built more drama into their capitols than might otherwise have been the case. Whatever the reason courthouses of that vintage have towers and cupolas and hidden circular stairwells—as at Waxahachie—rooms without entrance—such as the one at Clarksville—and doors leading nowhere. Originally Shelby County's useless door afforded the judge a means of escape. Center had an oversupply of rough customers when the architect provided a narrow stairway with a courtroom exit behind the bench, which kept the judge from encountering friends and relatives of men he had just sentenced to prison or worse. By 1926 the Moderator-Liberator country was sufficiently civilized to permit the exit to be boarded over and the outside door permanently locked.

The third courthouse would be a two or three story brick building. Opponents of the bond issue made necessary by the fact that the proposed structure cost more than its predecessors combined would charge the commissioners with putting on airs. An injunction might be sought, as when Wharton County was about to construct $25,000 of new courthouse in 1888. The bitterness generated by these controversies was intense—the Rangers had to be sent to Wharton—and colored subsequent issues for years. Wharton County citizens later feuded over the trees on the square. The county agent had planted pecans among the sycamores, hoping to stimulate interest in pecan raising. After the pecan trees were flourishing the commissioners decided the sycamores should go. The populace then split into angry pecan and sycamore factions. Finally it was agreed that the sycamores would remain, but citizens awoke one morning to find that persons unknown had cut down the sycamores so expertly that not one had fallen against a pecan tree.

The third building would have a dome or tower rising above homes and business buildings, as befitted a capitol. It would have a clock and bells and perhaps a statue. When Comanche County's statue of Justice was taken down she was found to have bullet holes in her neck, which was a surprise, although everyone knew that Will Baxter, demonstrating a new rifle stocked by Baxter Brothers New York Cash Store, had shot off the right arm. After that courthouse was demolished Comanche jewelers sold a lot of watches to people who had depended on the public clock. The Wharton *Spectator* commented on a similar loss. "It's not the same Wharton anymore. The old courthouse clock, the one which told a different story on each side of the building, and none of which was right, is gone . . . consternation reigns." Near the turn of the century electricity and indoor plumbing would be installed. The exposed wires and pipes would encourage sentiment for a new courthouse. Those proposing a change would make an inordinate use of the words modern and efficient.

The fourth courthouse would set new records for cost but would be diminished in adventure and imagination. The coming of age of the United States, the growth of business, the Spindletop discovery, and technology were factors working against the grand, monumental courthouse. The design of courthouses became more businesslike with each passing year, as the county's importance diminished while that of business and the federal government grew. The courthouse, once the largest structure in town, was equalled and then dwarfed by hotels and theaters.

When the fifth edifice was erected its cost was astronomical, but its design was pedestrian. There was no tower or dome: the capitol was no longer at the county seat but in Washington. The courthouse was simply a county office building and a place for trials to be held. Only its location on the square distinguished it from the home office of an insurance company.

The building of a courthouse had historical importance. Usually the Masonic lodge leveled the cornerstone, inside of which the builders sometimes left mementoes of themselves. A 37-year old bottle of sherry from the cornerstone of the Wharton County capitol was sent to Governor L. S. Ross in 1889. And the opening of the Eastland cornerstone in 1928 disclosed Old Rip, a live horned toad alleged to have been placed there 35 years before. Old Rip became a celebrity and was taken to Washington to be seen by President Calvin Coolidge. He lies in state at Eastland today.

In 1909, workmen excavating for a new Scurry County courthouse dug into the graves of a Ranger and his two nephews, killed there many years before. Rangers had pursued a Comanche war party from North Texas. Finally the Indians made a stand at Deep Creek, resulting in the deaths.

Sometimes there were construction difficulties. The contractor for Sweet-water's rock courthouse was asked by the commissioners to use locally manufactured plaster of paris in the mortar rather than lime and cement. Soon after the $20,000 courthouse was accepted in May, 1882, the mortar began to give way. After years of trying to patch the building, the Nolan County commissioners' minutes for April 15, 1891, noted that the "Courthouse having fallen down, no safe place for keeping records and preserving public records, necessary to rebuild new courthouse out of old material." It cost $12,935 to tear down and reconstruct the courthouse.

Materials for the second Castro County courthouse were hauled from Hereford by a freighter who pulled coupled wagons with a steam engine. The contraption was really an untracked freight train. Work on the courthouse was slowed because of a labor dispute. One of the employees removed the wheel nuts from the axles of the wagons and the freighter capitulated. The employee fished out of Hereford Creek a tow sack full of wheel nuts.

Jail facilities were usually separate from the early courthouses. Grayson County built its jail with no windows or doors. Prisoners were lowered and raised through a trap door on top, an arrangement similar to that used in Jeff Davis County where the jail was a dungeon beneath the Bat Cave, as the courthouse was affectionately called. Castro County jail facilities were so inadequate the sheriff sometimes ran into prisoners downtown, a minor problem since they always returned to their cells at mealtime and at night. A dangerous prisoner was another matter. One early sheriff kept the bad ones handcuffed to him even to the extent of taking them home and sleeping with them.

The early courthouses were well used. Castro County's unpartitioned second floor was fine for dances. A ladder nailed to the outside of the building led to the cupola, which cowboys used as a poker parlor, claiming it had the best breeze in town. The courthouse burned in 1906 after being struck by lightning. (Many courthouses burned. The Milam County capitol was destroyed about the same time as others in the area, giving rise to the theory that a forger was burning every courthouse containing his handiwork.)

An early Grayson County courthouse was literally used up and was sold to the highest bidder for $5. Courthouse squares accomodated picnics and barbecues and revivals. Collingsworth County's first capitol afforded relief from the flat country. Beneath the clock tower porticoes faced the points of the compass. An old timer wrote, "No young beau thought he had shown his girl the sights until he had taken her up on the courthouse balcony. Older men and women went up to get sight of the rolling prairie land, which was becoming a farming land as the years slipped by. Daring youngsters climbed up a rickety ladder from the balcony to the very top of the spire."

The courthouse was the only place in Randall County large enough to accomodate a crowd. Cowhands danced on the roof until their heels wore through the metal covering: the shingle roof replacement was unsuitable for dancing. Weddings and funerals were held there, but Christmas was the big event. The men would go into Palo Duro Canyon for a tree tall enough to touch the courthouse ceiling. (Paul Crume tells of similar doings in the treeless Lariat country, when a team and wagon, twenty-five men, and one axe disappeared for several days on the Christmas tree errand. Rumors would filter back that the men owned a jug and were having a high old time.) The women and children covered the tree with such homemade decorations as the High Plains afforded, and all of Randall County would meet in the courtroom to exchange presents and observe the Yuletide. The tree and celebration have moved out of the Texas courthouses—except for carolers who are an institution in Dallas County—but any number of county capitols leave their Christmas lights up all year round.

Another feature of the courthouse was its rest rooms, which probably were important to the loafers and were definitely counted upon by proprietors of an early Crowell movie theater. Its patrons had to cross the street to the Foard County capitol since the theater provided no facilities.

But the most important role of the courthouse was symbolic. The Wharton *Independent*, in 1888, noted, "It has been truly said that the glory of a people is inspired by the genius of their institutions, by the monuments they build and the edifices they erect . . . How meet it is then, in this era of progress, that we people of Wharton should set up in our gateway a structure that shall proclaim to the world our advanced ideas, our high conception of patriotism, and our love for the beautiful in art . . . Build, build high this temple of justice, that the virtues of our people may endure forever."

The Courthouses

Anderson County
Palestine

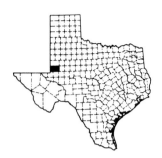

Andrews County
Andrews

Angelina County
Lufkin

Aransas County
Rockport

Archer County
Archer City

Armstrong County
Claude

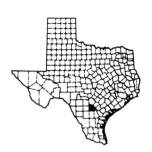

Atascosa County
Jourdanton

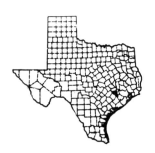

Austin County
Bellville

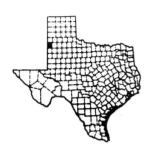

Bailey County
Muleshoe

23

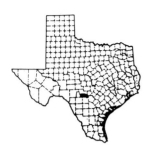

Bandera County
Bandera

Bastrop County
Bastrop

Baylor County
Seymour

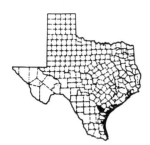

Bee County
Beeville

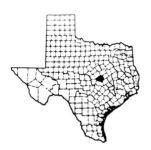

Bell County
Belton

Bexar County
San Antonio

Blanco County
Johnson City

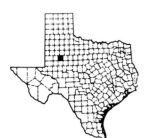

Borden County
Gail

Bosque County
Meridian

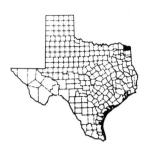

Bowie County
Boston

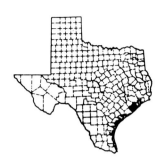

Brazoria County
Angleton

Brazos County
Bryan

35

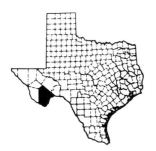

Brewster County
Alpine

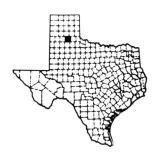

Briscoe County
Silverton

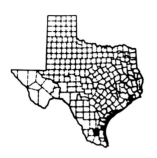

Brooks County
Falfurrias

Brown County
Brownwood

Burleson County
Caldwell

Burnet County
Burnet

41

Caldwell County
Lockhart

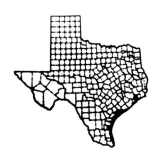

Calhoun County
Port Lavaca

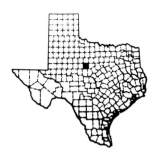

Callahan County
Baird

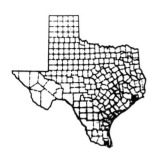

Cameron County
Brownsville

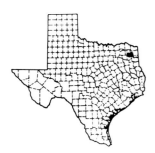

Camp County
Pittsburg

Carson County
Panhandle

Cass County
Linden

48

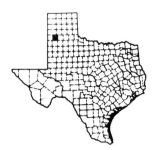

Castro County
Dimmitt

Chambers County
Anahuac

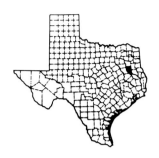

Cherokee County
Rusk

Childress County
Childress

Clay County
Henrietta

Cochran County
Morton

Coke County
Robert Lee

Coleman County
Coleman

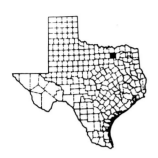

Collin County
McKinney

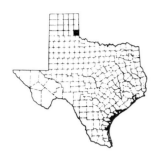

Collingsworth County
Wellington

58

Colorado County
Columbus

Comal County
New Braunfels

Comanche County
Comanche

Concho County
Paint Rock

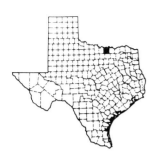

Cooke County
Gainesville

Coryell County
Gatesville

64

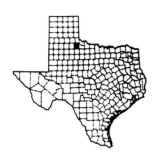

Cottle County
Paducah

Crane County
Crane

66

Crockett County
Ozona

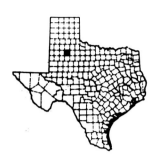

Crosby County
Crosbyton

Culberson County
Van Horn

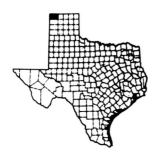

Dallam County
Dalhart

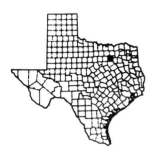

Dallas County
Dallas

Dawson County
Lamesa

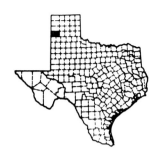

Deaf Smith County
Hereford

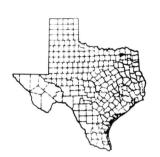

Delta County
Cooper

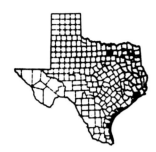

Denton County
Denton

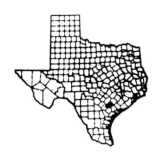

DeWitt County
Cuero

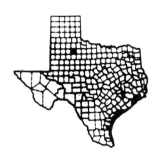

Dickens County
Dickens

Dimmitt County
Carrizo Springs

78

Donley County
Clarendon

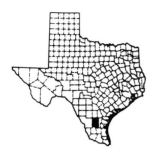

Duval County
San Diego

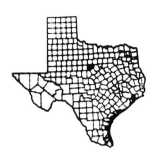

Eastland County
Eastland

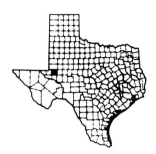

Ector County
Odessa

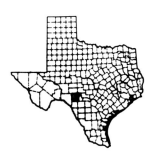

Edwards County
Rocksprings

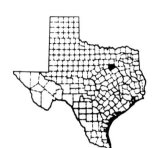

Ellis County
Waxahachie

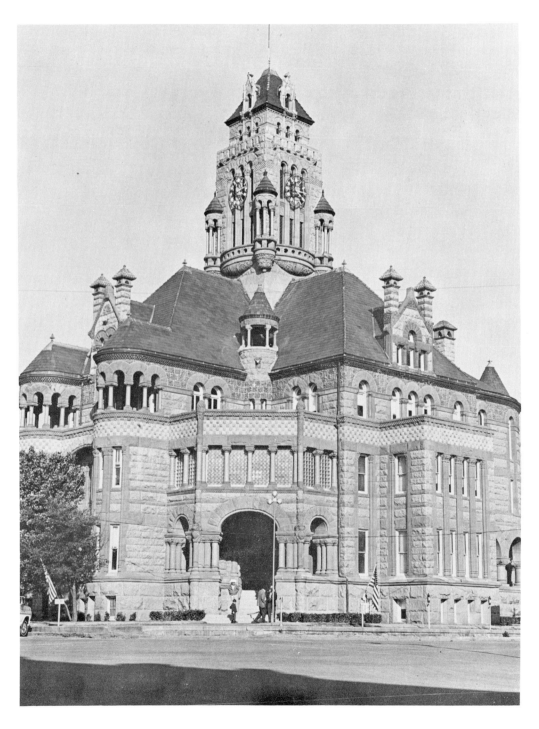

El Paso County
El Paso

Erath County
Stephenville

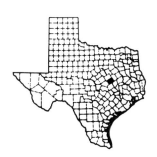

Falls County
Marlin

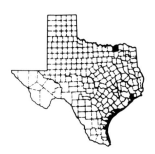

Fannin County
Bonham

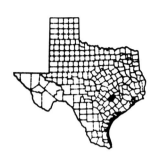

Fayette County
La Grange

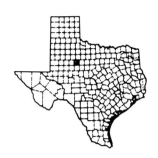

Fisher County
Roby

Floyd County
Floydada

Foard County
Crowell

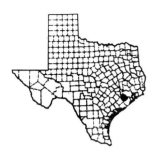

Fort Bend County
Richmond

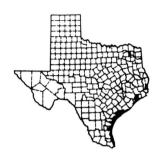

Franklin County
Mount Vernon

94

Freestone County
Fairfield

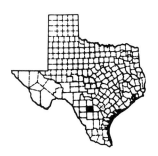

Frio County
Pearsall

96

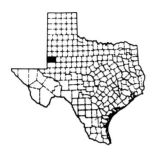

Gaines County
Seminole

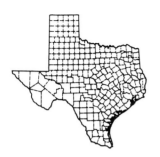

Galveston County
Galveston

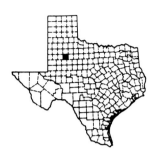

Garza County
Post

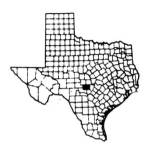

Gillespie County
Fredericksburg

Glasscock County
Garden City

101

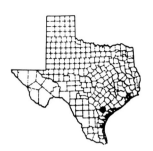

Goliad County
Goliad

Gonzales County
Gonzales

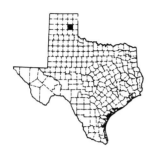

Gray County
Pampa

Grayson County
Sherman

Gregg County
Longview

Grimes County
Anderson

Guadalupe County
Seguin

Hale County
Plainview

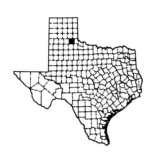

Hall County
Memphis

Hamilton County
Hamilton

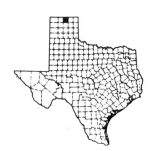

Hansford County
Spearman

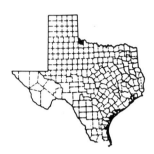

Hardeman County
Quanah

Hardin County
Kountze

Harris County
Houston

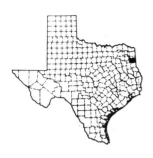

Harrison County
Marshall

Hartley County
Channing

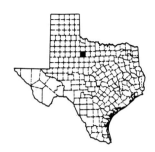

Haskell County
Haskell

118

Hays County
San Marcos

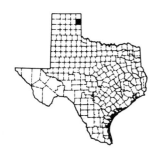

Hemphill County
Canadian

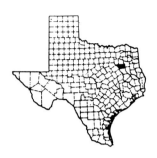

Henderson County
Athens

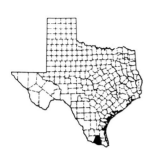

Hidalgo County
Edinburg

Hill County
Hillsboro

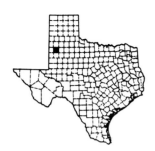

Hockley County
Levelland

124

Hood County
Granbury

125

Hopkins County
Sulphur Springs

Houston County
Crockett

Howard County
Big Spring

Hudspeth County
Sierra Blanca

Hunt County
Greenville

Hutchinson County
Stinnett

Irion County
Mertzon

Jack County
Jacksboro

Jackson County
Edna

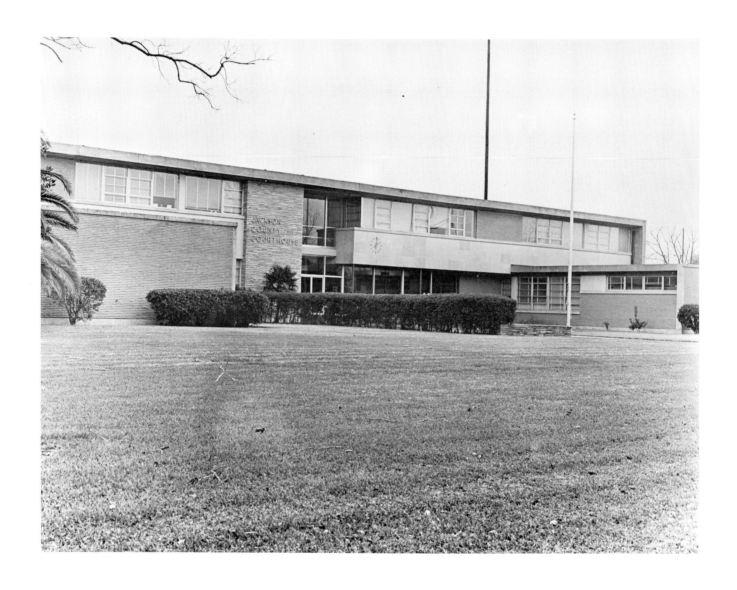

134

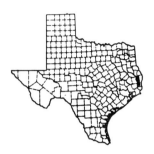

Jasper County
Jasper

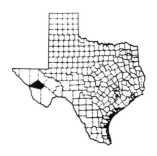

Jeff Davis County
Fort Davis

Jefferson County
Beaumont

Jim Hogg County
Hebbronville

Jim Wells County
Alice

Johnson County
Cleburne

140

Jones County
Anson

Karnes County
Karnes City

Old Helena Courthouse

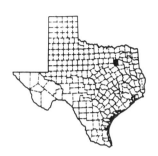

Kaufman County
Kaufman

Kendall County
Boerne

144

Kenedy County
Sarita

145

Kent County
Jayton

146

Kerr County
Kerrville

Kimble County
Junction

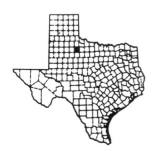

King County
Guthrie

Kinney County
Brackettville

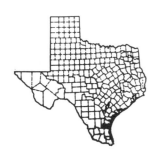

Kleberg County
Kingsville

Knox County
Benjamin

Lamar County
Paris

Lamb County
Littlefield

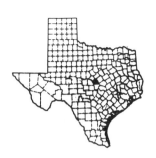

Lampasas County
Lampasas

La Salle County
Cotulla

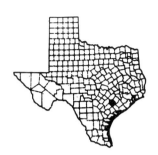

Lavaca County
Hallettsville

157

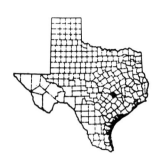

Lee County
Giddings

158

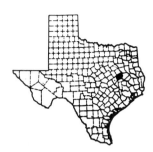

Leon County
Centerville

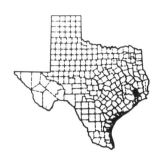

Liberty County
Liberty

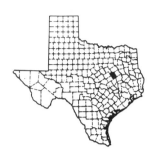

Limestone County
Groesbeck

161

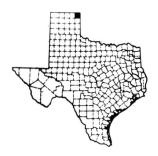

Lipscomb County
Lipscomb

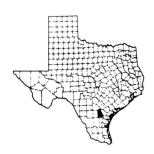

Live Oak County
George West

Llano County
Llano

164

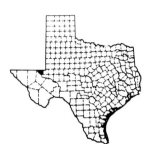

Loving County
Mentone

Lubbock County
Lubbock

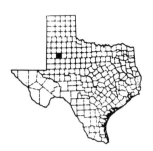

Lynn County
Tahoka

167

McCulloch County
Brady

McLennan County
Waco

169

McMullen County
Tilden

170

Madison County
Madisonville

Marion County
Jefferson

172

Martin County
Stanton

Mason County
Mason

174

Matagorda County
Bay City

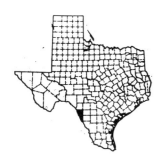

Maverick County
Eagle Pass

176

Medina County
Hondo

Menard County
Menard

Midland County
Midland

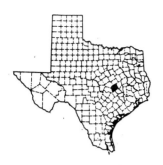

Milam County
Cameron

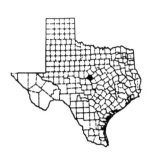

Mills County
Goldthwaite

Mitchell County
Colorado City

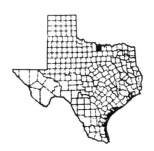

Montague County
Montague

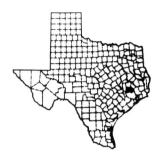

Montgomery County
Conroe

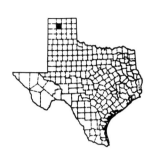

Moore County
Dumas

185

Morris County
Daingerfield

186

Motley County
Matador

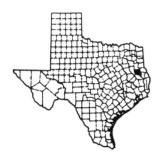

Nacogdoches County
Nacogdoches

Navarro County
Corsicana

Newton County
Newton

Nolan County
Sweetwater

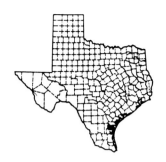

Nueces County
Corpus Christi

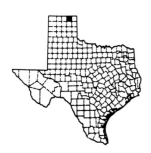

Ochiltree County
Perryton

Oldham County
Vega

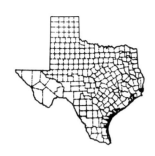

Orange County
Orange

Palo Pinto County
Palo Pinto

Panola County
Carthage

Parker County
Weatherford

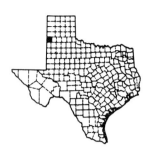

Parmer County
Farwell

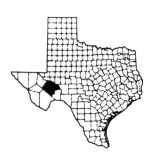

Pecos County
Fort Stockton

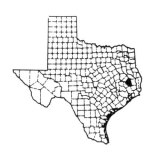

Polk County
Livingston

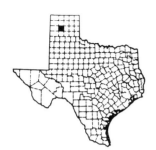

Potter County
Amarillo

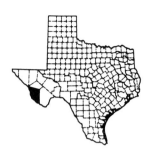

Presidio County
Marfa

Rains County
Emory

Randall County
Canyon

Reagan County
Big Lake

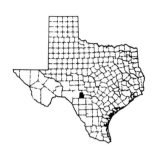

Real County
Leakey

Red River County
Clarksville

Reeves County
Pecos

Refugio County
Refugio

Roberts County
Miami

Robertson County
Franklin

Rockwall County
Rockwall

Runnels County
Ballinger

Rusk County
Henderson

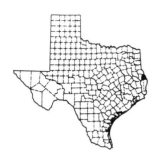

Sabine County
Hemphill

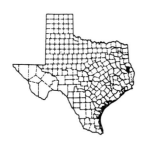

San Augustine County
San Augustine

San Jacinto County
Coldspring

San Patricio County
Sinton

San Saba County
San Saba

Schleicher County
El Dorado

**Scurry County
Snyder**

222

Shackelford County
Albany

Shelby County
Center

Sherman County
Stratford

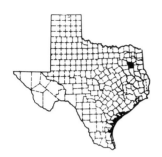

Smith County
Tyler

Somervell County
Glen Rose

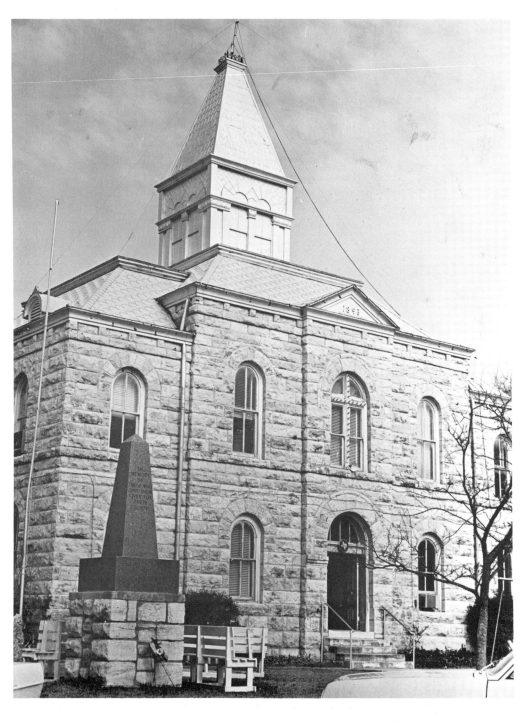

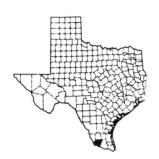

Starr County
Rio Grande City

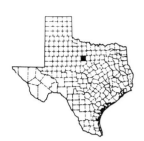

Stephens County
Breckenridge

Sterling County
Sterling City

Stonewall County
Aspermont

Sutton County
Sonora

Swisher County
Tulia

Tarrant County
Fort Worth

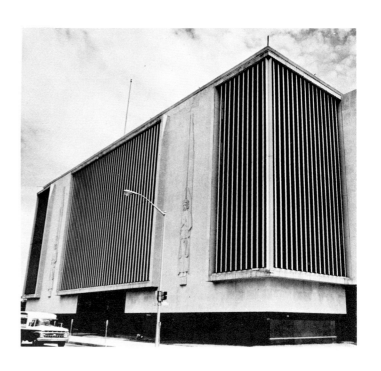

Taylor County
Abilene

235

Terrell County
Sanderson

236

Terry County
Brownfield

Throckmorton County
Throckmorton

Titus County
Mount Pleasant

Tom Green County
San Angelo

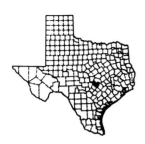

Travis County
Austin

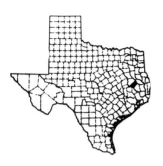

Trinity County
Groveton

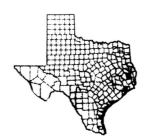

Tyler County
Woodville

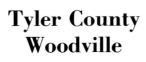

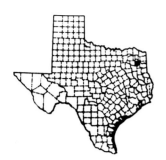

Upshur County
Gilmer

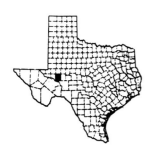

Upton County
Rankin

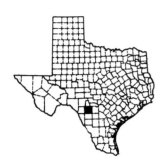

Uvalde County
Uvalde

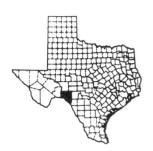

Val Verde County
Del Rio

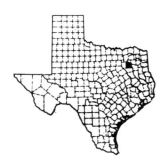

Van Zandt County
Canton

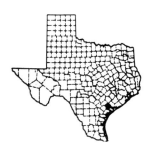

Victoria County
Victoria

**Walker County
Huntsville**

Waller County
Hempstead

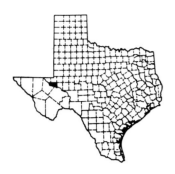

Ward County
Monahans

Washington County
Brenham

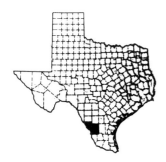

Webb County
Laredo

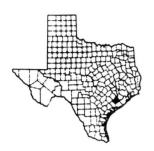

Wharton County
Wharton

Wheeler County
Wheeler

Wichita County
Wichita Falls

Wilbarger County
Vernon

Willacy County
Raymondville

Williamson County
Georgetown

Wilson County
Floresville

Winkler County
Kermit

Wise County
Decatur

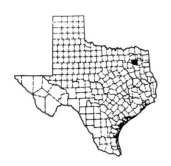

Wood County
Quitman

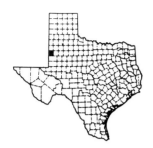

Yoakum County
Plains

Young County
Graham

Zapata County
Zapata

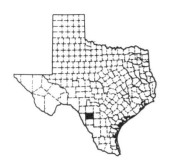

Zavala County
Crystal City

The Counties

ANDERSON COUNTY, PALESTINE. Kenneth Lewis Anderson, a native of North Carolina, settled at San Augustine in 1837. During the Republic he was speaker of the House, district attorney, and Anson Jones' vice president. Later he resided at Fanthorp, Grimes County: it was renamed Anderson in his honor.

Daniel Parker began the first settlement in the county in 1833. Parker, a primitive Baptist minister, established at Elkhart the old Pilgrim Church, probably the oldest Protestant church in Texas.

The first Anderson County courthouse was used until a two-story frame structure was completed in 1847. A red brick courthouse costing some $6,000 was built in 1885. It was surrounded by a tall plank fence. In the middle eighties a Victorian courthouse was constructed. The $40,500 cost so upset the voters that most of the commissioners were defeated at the next election. Work on the present courthouse was begun in July, 1912, after its predecessor burned. It was completed in 1914 and cost $200,000.

ANDREWS COUNTY, ANDREWS. Richard Andrews' father was one of Stephen Austin's first colonists. When the revolution began Richard Andrews was at Gonzales. He was killed at the Battle of Concepción October 23, 1835, the first Texan to die in the war. Noah Smithwick said, ". . . the foolhardiness of some of our men caused the only casualty of the engagement . . . I ran to him and attempted to raise him. 'Dick,' I cried, 'are you hurt?' 'Yes, Smith,' he replied, 'I'm killed; lay me down.' "

Andrews County was created in 1876, but was not organized until 1910. The population in 1890 was 24. In the next decade it increased to 87.

The present courthouse, built in 1939 at a cost of $110,000 is the county's second. A 1955 addition cost $425,000 and another, in 1960, $225,000.

ANGELINA COUNTY, LUFKIN. The Angelina River, which borders Angelina County on the northeast, commemorates Angelina, an Hasinai Indian girl of such intelligence that she was taken from her East Texas home to be educated at the Mission San Juan Bautista on the Rio Grande. In the early 18th century she acted as an interpreter for Spaniards and Frenchmen traveling in East Texas.

The first settlers, in 1834, found Shawnee and Cherokee Indians there as well as the native Caddoes. The county was created in 1846 with Marion the capital. Jonesville became the county seat in 1854, then Homer in 1858, and finally Lufkin in 1892. The present $650,000 courthouse, completed in 1955, is the county's fifth.

ARANSAS COUNTY, ROCKPORT. The Aransas River—El Rio Nuestra Señora de Aranzazu—empties into Copano Bay from Aransas County. Diego Ortiz Parilla passed through the county in 1766, but no settlement was made until 1829 when the Irish empresarios James Power and James Hewetson brought colonists from Ireland.

Rockport, which began as a shipping point for beef products such as tallow, hides, and bones—lack of refrigeration precluded shipment of meat—was the seat of Refugio County until 1871 when it became the capital of the new Aransas County. The present courthouse is Aransas County's third and was built in 1956 at a cost of $480,000.

ARCHER COUNTY, ARCHER CITY. Branch T. Archer, a physician and former member of the Virginia House of Burgesses, was active in the Texas Revolution. He, Stephen F. Austin, and William H. Wharton were sent to the United States to seek financing for the Texan cause. He was later speaker of the House of the Republic.

Archer County was created in 1858, when there was no white population. Dr. R. O. Prideaux, English-born and educated in Scotland, settled there in 1874. His wife was a native of Sweden. Cattle ranching was impossible while the buffalo remained. He raised hogs until the buffalo were gone, walking them to market in Fort Worth.

The county was organized in 1880. The present courthouse, built in 1891 for $36,500, was remodeled in 1925, at which time one story was added and the mansard roof and an ornate tower removed.

ARMSTRONG COUNTY, CLAUDE. Both the *Handbook of Texas* and the *Texas Almanac* state that Armstrong County was named for a pioneer family, but in *A History of Armstrong County* a citizen of the county says, "Why the name Armstrong? We wonder. It is said that in the counties formed by the paper survey that names of people who were prominent in the state were drawn and placed on new county spaces at random. Our county had the name Armstrong placed on it." By "paper survey" the writer refers to the legislature's simply drawing lines approximately 30 miles apart on a Texas map in 1876, creating in that fashion Armstrong and 53 other counties.

Charlie Goodnight was the first settler, establishing his ranch in Palo Duro Canyon in 1876. The county was organized in 1890. The first courthouse was a two-story frame building. The existing courthouse, the third, was built in 1912 at a cost of $40,000.

ATASCOSA COUNTY, JOURDANTON. The Atascosa River traverses Atascosa County. Atascosa means boggy, coming from the Spanish verb "atascarse," which means "to mire" or "to bog". José Antonio Navarro was granted land by Mexico, in 1828, and the Republic of Texas. He donated the site for the first county seat, Navatasco, in 1857. A log courthouse was built, but because of Indian raids in 1858 the county seat was moved to a location which became Pleasanton. A courthouse was constructed for $125. After nine years of use the school trustees rented it for $15 a month and a new courthouse was built. The first jail was a hole 12 feet deep, roofed and with a padlocked trap door.

Jourdan Campbell founded Jourdanton in 1909 as part of a plan to get the Artesian Belt Railroad to come into that part of Atascosa County. Within a year Jourdanton was the county seat. The present courthouse was built in 1912.

AUSTIN COUNTY, BELLVILLE. Stephen F. Austin's capital, San Felipe, is in Austin County. It was established in 1823 and was the unofficial headquarters of American immigrants. San Felipe was burned during the revolution, then rebuilt. It was the seat of Austin County until 1846 when it was succeeded by Bellville. The present courthouse, Austin County's fourth, was built in 1960 at a cost of $511,918 after the 1886 courthouse burned.

BAILEY COUNTY, MULESHOE. The county was created in 1876 and named for Alamo defender Peter J. Bailey. The Muleshoe Ranch and part of the XIT were located in the county, which did not have enough people to organize until

1917. The Masonic Lodge Hall in Muleshoe served as the courthouse until the present $80,000 structure was built in 1925.

BANDERA COUNTY, BANDERA. In about 1720, a General Bandera—bandera means flag or banner—was sent after Apaches who had been raiding San Antonio. He chased them out of present Bandera County. Bandera Pass, Bandera Mountains, and Bandera Creek were named for him. The county and town took the name of the mountains. The first settlers arrived in 1852. They made cypress shingles on the Medina River for sale in San Antonio. Some Mormons settled at Bandera in 1854. In the next year a colony of Poles arrived after first having stopped at Panna Maria.

Bandera County was organized in 1856. The first courthouse still stands. The present courthouse, begun in 1887, was designed by B. F. Lester, Jr. of San Antonio, who was paid $50 for his work and who died while it was in progress. The contractors quit before the job was accepted, were penalized $360 for a 96-day delay, and the county commissioners finished the $20,000 building.

BASTROP COUNTY, BASTROP. Felipe Enrique Neri, the Baron de Bastrop, enabled Moses Austin to get his colonization grant and then assisted Stephen F. Austin in establishing his colonists. Born in Holland, the Baron was a soldier in the army of Frederick the Great, served in the Spanish Army, and in his last years was a member of the legislature of Texas y Coahuila. He died in 1827, so impoverished that fellow legislators had to take up a collection for his burial expenses.

Permanent settlement began in 1829. Organized in 1837, Bastrop was one of the original 23 counties of the Republic. Bastrop, the county seat, was originally named Mina, although early resident Noah Smithwick wrote that he did not remember the town's bearing that name.

The first Bastrop courthouse, built in 1840, was called the Meeting House. The second courthouse was situated on property purchased from Pinckney Hill for a slave girl and a mule. The third capitol was located east of Main Street. It served until 1853, when a courthouse was built on the present site: after it burned the present courthouse was erected in 1883 at a cost of $33,000. An addition was constructed in 1953.

BAYLOR COUNTY, SEYMOUR. Kentuckian Henry W. Baylor fought Texas Indians before studying medicine at Transylvania University in Kentucky. During the Mexican War he was a surgeon in Jack Hays' regiment and then raised his own Ranger company in Fayette County.

Baylor County was buffalo country long after it was created in 1858. Ranchers and cattle succeeded the Indians and buffalo. The drovers' Western Trail crossed the immigrant trail to California near present Seymour, which was originally Oregon City. Because of another Texas town of similar name Oregon City, in 1878, became Seymour, honoring Seymour Munday, a cowhand. There was fighting as ranchers sought to keep the farmers out. In 1881, two years after organization, County Judge G. R. Morris was killed at a stormy meeting of the commissioners court. The present courthouse, Baylor County's second, cost $350,000 in 1968 and replaced a $50,000 native stone building erected in 1884.

BEE COUNTY, BEEVILLE. Barnard Bee, of South Carolina who served in the Texas Army, was secretary of state under presidents David G. Burnet and M. B. Lamar and was Sam Houston's secretary of war.

The first settlers, in 1826, were Irishmen Jeremiah O'Tool, his sons, and James O'Reilly. The county was organized in 1858. The first county seat was Beeville. When the county government moved to Maryville, in 1860, Maryville's name was changed to Beeville. Residents called the first capital Beeville-on-the-Medio and the second Beeville-on-the-Poesta. The first courthouse cost $160 and was built "picket fence style, with clapboard roof and dirt floor." At Beeville-on-the-Poesta, a $750 courthouse was erected south of the present Commercial National Bank Building. Then a $3,425 frame courthouse built on the present site in 1878 burned in 1911. The county offered a thousand dollar reward for the arsonist. The present Bee County courthouse was occupied in 1912 and cost $72,000. A wing was added in 1942, and the entire structure was remodeled in 1950.

BELL COUNTY, BELTON. Peter Hansborough Bell, a Virginian, fought at San Jacinto, was a Ranger, a major in the Somervell Expedition, an officer in the Mexican War, governor of Texas, a congressman, and a Confederate colonel.

Some settlement occurred in the early thirties, but the Runaway Scrape depopulated the county in 1836. Those who returned after San Jacinto were forced out again that year by Indians. George Erath built a fort in late 1836, but Indian trouble caused abandonment of the county in 1838. Resettlement began after 1843 and Bell county was organized in 1850. Nolanville, the county seat, became Belton in 1851. Bell County's third courthouse was built in 1884 at a cost of $64,965.

BEXAR COUNTY, SAN ANTONIO. At the time of the founding of the mission San Antonio de Valero and the presidio San Antonio de Bexar, in 1718, the Spanish viceroy was Balthasar Manuel de Zuñiga y Guzman Sotomayor y Sarmiento, the second son of the Duke of Bexar. Canary Islands colonists founded the villa San Fernando in 1731, the first civil settlement in Texas. San Fernando de Bexar became the capital of Texas in 1773. Bexar County, formed in 1836, was huge: 128 counties were created from it.

The first courthouse—also the first public building in Texas—was the Casas Reales-Council House that served from 1731 into the 1840's. The next courthouse, Mason's Building, was used during the forties and fifties. The third, the Bat Cave, was in use from the fifties to 1890. The present courthouse was built in 1892 and enlarged in 1928.

BLANCO COUNTY, JOHNSON CITY. Blanco County was named for the Blanco River, which may have meant the White River or may have honored Victor Blanco, governor of Coahuila y Texas in 1826.

The county was organized in 1858 with Blanco the seat of government. A $600 courthouse was built there. Union sympathizers formed Kendall County out of Blanco County in 1861, with the result that Blanco was no longer in the center of the county. Johnson City was founded in 1879 and after a decade of controversy Johnson City became the county seat in 1891. The present courthouse is Blanco County's fifth and cost $34,000 in 1916.

BORDEN COUNTY, GAIL. Gail Borden, born in New York, taught school in

Mississippi before he came to Texas in 1830. He was Austin's secretary for awhile and he published the first newspaper in Houston, a city he had helped survey and plat. He founded the Borden Company to market milk condensed by a technique he devised.

As late as 1880, the population of Borden County was only 35. It was organized 10 years later when there were 222 residents. The second Borden County courthouse cost some $40,000 and was built in 1939.

BOSQUE COUNTY, MERIDIAN. The county is named after the Bosque River. In Spanish bosque means woods. Bosque County was part of the Sterling C. Robertson colony. Most of the Norwegians who came to Texas settled there.

Bosque County was organized in 1854. The present $60,000 courthouse was built in 1886 and is Bosque County's fourth: all were located at Meridian, which was laid out by George B. Erath. Meridian's first building was the 1854 log courthouse.

BOWIE COUNTY, BOSTON. James Bowie, of Tennessee, moved to Louisiana where he is alleged to have ridden alligators. He smuggled slaves, sometimes with the pirate Jean Lafitte. He was wounded near Natchez in the Sandbar Duel, where the duelists settled their problems peacefully but an altercation developed among the spectators. He designed the Bowie knife after the weapon he used in the Sandbar Duel. He died at the Alamo March 6, 1836.

Settlement in Bowie County preceded that in the Austin Colony: Ben Milam arrived there about 1819. Bowie County was organized in 1840 with Boston, then about three miles from its present location, the county seat. A survey revealed that Boston was not within five miles of the center of the county, as required by law. Boston was moved to its present site, and the other town became Old Boston. After the railroad was built north of Boston the town which grew up on the right of way was called New Boston. The existing courthouse was built in 1889, remodeled in 1937, and expanded in 1951.

BRAZORIA COUNTY, ANGLETON. Brazoria County, at the mouth of the Brazos River, was Karankawa country when 71 of Austin's first colonists settled there. The municipality of Brazoria was created out of the San Felipe municipality in 1832.

Brazoria County was one of the original counties of the Republic. Brazoria, which had been the principal town of the Mexican municipality, was the county seat until 1897 when it was succeeded by Angleton. The present $500,000 courthouse, Brazoria County's fourth, was completed in 1940. Its immediate predecessor, built in 1897, is still used for county business.

BRAZOS COUNTY, BRYAN. Brazos County lies between the Brazos and Navasota Rivers and was part of Austin's second colony. The county was created during the Republic and called Navasota County. Upon organization in 1843 the name was changed to Brazos County. Boonville was the capital until Bryan, built on the Houston and Texas Central Railroad, became the county seat in 1866. Four courthouses preceded the present one, which was completed in 1965 and cost some $800,000.

BREWSTER COUNTY, ALPINE. After fighting at San Jacinto, Henry P.

Brewster, of South Carolina, was David G. Burnet's secretary of war. Later he was the Texas attorney general and during the Civil War was General Albert Sidney Johnston's chief of staff.

Brewster is the largest county, covering 6,208 square miles. It was part of Santa Fe County, which never functioned, and then part of Presidio County.

Brewster County was organized in 1887 with the county seat at Murpheyville, which became Alpine. An early description of Alpine was, "Three buildings surrounded by solitude..." The original courthouse is still in use. It cost $35,000 in 1887 and was renovated in 1934.

BRISCOE COUNTY, SILVERTON. Andrew Briscoe of Mississippi was an Anahuac merchant. In 1835 he and DeWitt Clinton Harris were jailed for trying to trade goods on which customs duties had not been paid. W. B. Travis and others forced the Mexican commander to release them. Briscoe followed Ben Milam into Bexar and fought in the battles of Concepción and San Jacinto.

Charles Goodnight bought the Quitaque Ranch, which was headquartered in Briscoe County, for John Adair in 1882. Although created in 1876, the county was not organized until 1892, five years after the arrival of the railroad. Silverton has always been the county seat. One courthouse preceded the present $70,000 structure, which was built in 1922 and renovated in 1954.

BROOKS COUNTY, FALFURRIAS. Kentuckian James A. Brooks was a Ranger captain from 1889 to 1906. Then he moved to Falfurrias, was a member of the legislature, and was judge of the county named for him from 1911 until 1939.

Little development occurred in the county until the twentieth century. The Texas and New Orleans Railroad reached the area in 1903: mail had been brought on horseback prior to that. Brooks County was organized in 1912. The original courthouse, completed in 1914 at a cost of $80,000, is still is use.

BROWN COUNTY, BROWNWOOD. Henry Stevenson Brown, of Kentucky, a veteran of the War of 1812 and a Missouri sheriff, came to Texas in 1824. A company of settlers led by him defeated a band of Waco Indians on the site of modern Waco. He was active in events leading to the revolution, but died in 1834.

Brown County was organized in 1858. The population was 200. Because of its exposed position, after 20 years there were fewer than 600 inhabitants. The first courthouse was a log cabin 1 1/2 miles east of the present location. The courthouse was moved because a decent well could not be had at the first site. In 1865 a second story was added to the building to serve as a Masonic Lodge. When title to the land proved defective, the courthouse was moved to its current location. The present courthouse, Brown County's fourth, was completed in 1917 and cost $85,000.

BURLESON COUNTY, CALDWELL. Edward Burleson, a North Carolinian who settled in Austin's second colony in 1830, commanded the Texan Army at the seige of Bexar after Austin was ordered to seek aid in the United States. Burleson fought at San Jacinto, was a member of the Texian Congress, and in 1838 laid out the city of Austin, at that time called Waterloo. He was an Indian fighter, vice president of the Republic, and a soldier in the Mexican War.

There was settlement in the county as early as 1825. When Burleson County was organized in 1846 Caldwell, which had been the seat of Milam County, became the capital, and Cameron was founded to serve Milam County. The present $200,000 courthouse was completed in 1927.

BURNET COUNTY, BURNET. David G. Burnet of New Jersey took part in Francisco de Miranda's attempt to free Venezuela from Spain in 1806. In 1813 he established a trading post at Nachitoches, Louisiana. The business did not prosper, and having contracted tuberculosis he came to Texas. He fell sick and was cared for by the Comanches, with whom he lived for two years. In 1826 an empresario contract was granted to Lorenzo de Zavala, Joseph Vehlein, and Burnet. He was president of the ad interim government of Texas in 1836 and was Lamar's vice president. When Lamar resigned, December 13, 1841, Burnet was again, briefly, president of the Republic. After annexation he was secretary of state.

Settlement began in 1848. Two years later Mormons established a colony. Burnet County was organized in 1854. Two courthouses preceded the current one, built in 1936 at a cost of about $225,000.

CALDWELL COUNTY, LOCKHART. Kentuckian Mathew Caldwell, usually called Old Paint, signed the Texas Declaration of Independence, but is best known as an Indian fighter. He was wounded at the Council House Fight in March, 1840, and was one of the commanders at the Plum Creek battle near present Lockhart. As a member of the Santa Fe Expedition he was imprisoned in Mexico.

Caldwell County was organized in 1848. The name of the county seat, Plum Creek, was changed to Lockhart since Byrd Lockhart originally owned the site. Two courthouses preceded the present one, which cost $54,950 in 1894: Weldon Hart says that citizens objected to spending too much for the building. After the broom closets were converted into rest rooms the first month's water bill was so high the county judge padlocked the new facilities.

CALHOUN COUNTY, PORT LAVACA. Calhoun County honors Vice President John C. Calhoun of South Carolina. La Salle landed in Calhoun County in 1685. Linnville, the first settlement, was established in 1831, but was wiped out by Comanches in 1840.

The county was created in 1846. The county seat, Lavaca, was succeeded by Indianola in the fifties. Indianola had a population of about 6,000 at its peak, but after a bad hurricane and the diversion of water shipping because of Galveston's rail connections, Indianola began to decline. After another bad hurricane in 1886 the county government returned to Lavaca, called Port Lavaca by then. Indianola became a ghost town. The first courthouse, in Indianola, was built in 1857. The second was completed in 1887 at Port Lavaca. The third was erected in 1911, and the present million dollar facility was finished in 1959.

CALLAHAN COUNTY, BAIRD. James Hughes Callahan, of Georgia, was at the Battle of Coleto and was taken prisoner with the rest of Fannin's command. His life was spared in the Goliad Massacre because the Mexicans needed his services as a mechanic. In 1855, he took three Ranger companies after Lipan Apaches and Kickapoos, the pursuit extending into Mexico. The Rangers dismissed him for burning the town of Piedras Negras as he retreated from Mexico.

Callahan County was organized in 1877 with the capital at Belle Plain. Baird, which grew up on the Texas and Pacific right of way, became the county seat in 1880 after the railroad missed Belle Plain. Three courthouses preceded the present one, which cost $122,000 in 1929.

CAMERON COUNTY, BROWNSVILLE. Ewen Cameron, born in Scotland in 1811, took part in the Texas Revolution. He was a leader of the Mier Expedition in 1842 and headed an unsuccessful escape attempt by those taken prisoner at Mier. After the Mexicans recaptured the escapees, every tenth man was ordered shot. Those who would die were those who drew black beans from a jar. Cameron drew a white bean but Santa Anna had him shot anyway because he had planned the escape.

Cameron County was the first place Spaniards explored in Texas. Alonso Alvarez de Piñeda spent forty days at the mouth of the Rio Grande 452 years ago. Settlement by Americans began in 1845. Fort Brown was established in 1846 when Zachary Taylor's army established itself across the Rio Grande from Matamoras, Mexico. The fort was named for Major Jacob Brown who was killed early in the war. Cameron County was organized in 1848 with Brownsville, which had grown up next to the fort, the county seat. One courthouse existed prior to the present one, built in 1912 for $250,000.

CAMP COUNTY, PITTSBURG. Jean Lafayette Camp, of Alabama, practiced law at Gilmer. He was a Confederate colonel, twice wounded and twice captured. He was elected to Congress, but the radicals refused to seat him. Later, President Grover Cleveland appointed him land commissioner for Arizona.

Camp County was created out of Upshur County and organized in 1874 with Pittsburg the capital. The present courthouse, the third, cost $79,623.40 in 1928.

CARSON COUNTY, PANHANDLE. Samuel Carson was a North Carolina congressman who settled in Northeast Texas, signed the Declaration of Independence, and was secretary of state of the Republic.

Carson County was organized in 1888 with Carson City the county seat. Carson City became Panhandle. In 1889, the first courthouse cost $3,969. In 1901, a new courthouse and jail were built for $15,000. The third, in 1909, cost $40,000. The present $465,000 courthouse was completed in 1950.

CASS COUNTY, LINDEN. More than one state honored Senator Lewis Cass of Michigan by naming a county for him. Texans appreciated his support of annexation. In 1861 the name of the county was changed to Davis honoring the Confederate president, but after a decade the Cass name was restored.

Cass County was carved out of Bowie County in 1848. Jefferson was the county seat until about 1852 when the courthouse was built at Linden, a two-story frame building which was sold to a Baptist church in 1859. The present courthouse was completed in March, 1861, at a cost of $9,877. Additions were made about 1900, and a 1917 remodeling gave the building its present appearance.

CASTRO COUNTY, DIMMITT. Henri Castro, born in France, was of Portuguese descent. He brought a large number of European families to Texas, establishing settlements at Castroville and elsewhere.

Fourteen years after Castro County was created the 1890 census showed its population to be only nine. To get the required 150 names on an organization petition, citizens of Castro County committed a fraud: the petition for organization contained names of horses and non-residents. The county was organized in 1891 and a courthouse was built at Dimmitt the following year. It burned in 1906 and a one-story frame building served until a new courthouse was finished in 1908. The present edifice was completed in 1940 at a cost of some $90,000. In 1969 bonds were voted to pay for some $400,000 in improvements, doubling the floor space, remodeling the older portion, and installing air conditioning.

CHAMBERS COUNTY, ANAHUAC. Thomas Jefferson Chambers was a Virginian who became surveyor general of the State of Coahuila and Texas in 1829. As a reserve major general of the Texas Army, he was ordered to the United States to obtain supplies and raise volunteers. He was an unsuccessful candidate for governor four times, and he served in the secession convention. He was assassinated at his Anahuac home in 1865.

Settlement began in 1821. A fort was located at Anahuac as colonization was commenced, and Anahuac figured in most of the early troubles with Mexico.

Chambers County was created and organized in 1858 with Wallisville the county seat. A masonry structure was erected in 1876 to replace the frame courthouse that burned the year before. Anahuac became the county seat in 1908. The present courthouse was built in 1936 at a cost of $240,000.

CHEROKEE COUNTY, RUSK. Most of the Cherokees moving out of the southeastern states relocated in the Indian Territory, but some settled on the Neches River in 1832, encouraged by the governor of Coahuila y Texas who saw them as a buffer between Mexican settlement and the renegades of the old neutral ground in western Louisiana. The Indians were never able to get titles to the land they settled. In 1839 troops sent by President Lamar and commanded by General Rusk drove them out and they settled in the Indian Territory.

Cherokee County was organized in 1846. Rusk was the county seat. There were at least three courthouses before the present one, which was completed in 1941. The Works Project Administration furnished labor and some material, and the county paid $80,000 of the cost.

CHILDRESS COUNTY, CHILDRESS. The Texas Declaration of Independence was authored by George Campbell Childress, of Tennessee, a nephew of Sterling C. Robertson. In 1836, Childress and Robert Hamilton were sent to Washington to seek recognition. He died by his own hand at Galveston in 1841, at which time he was a candidate for the presidency of the Republic.

Childress County was organized in 1887, the year of the arrival of the Fort Worth and Denver Railroad. The 1887 courthouse burned about 1891. The present $250,000 courthouse was erected in 1939 and is the third for the county.

CLAY COUNTY, HENRIETTA. The county, named for Henry Clay, was created from Cooke County in 1857. It had a population of 109 in the 1860 census, but Indian raids were so bad during the Civil War that the county had to be abandoned. After the war a Dr. Eldridge brought in several families. They lived in houses abandoned by the earlier settlers until the Indians drove them out also. The 1870 census showed no population for the county.

Clay County was again organized in 1873. Cambridge was the capital until 1882 when the railroad made Henrietta the most important town in the county. Henrietta is supposed to have been named for Henry Clay's wife, but that was not her name. Probably someone decided Henrietta was Henry's feminine equivalent. The county had one courthouse before the present one was built in 1884 at a cost of $40,000.

COCHRAN COUNTY, MORTON. Robert Cochran, of New Jersey, was a resident of Brazoria when he joined the army. He died at the Alamo March 6, 1836.

The county was created in 1876 but not organized for almost half a century. Its population was 25 in 1900, all cowhands. A decade later Cochran County had 75 residents, and 67 in 1920. It was finally organized in 1924 with Morton the county seat. The next year came oil prospecting and the railroad. The county's only courthouse was built in 1926. In 1968, $360,000 was spent remodeling and enlarging it.

COKE COUNTY, ROBERT LEE. Governor Richard Coke followed the reconstruction governor E. J. Davis. A Virginian and a graduate of the College of William and Mary, Coke practiced law at Waco, became a Confederate captain, and was removed from the Texas Supreme Court by General Philip Sheridan as an "impediment to reconstruction." After his service as governor, he was a United States Senator for 18 years.

Robert Lee was named by a couple of Confederate veterans for General Robert E. Lee. The county was organized in 1889. Hayrick was the first county seat, succeeded by Robert Lee in 1891. Most Hayrick residents and businesses moved to Robert Lee. The present courthouse cost $300,000 in 1956, and is Coke County's third.

COLEMAN COUNTY, COLEMAN. Robert M. Coleman, a Kentuckian, captained a company at the seige of Bexar, signed the Declaration of Independence, and fought at San Jacinto. Later he commanded a regiment of Rangers. He drowned in the Brazos near Velasco.

Coleman County was organized in 1862 in an area that had grazed antelope, buffalo, and mustangs. The county seat was Camp Colorado on Jim Ned Creek. Camp Colorado had been built by the United States Army but had served Confederates and Rangers between periods of abandonment. In 1876 the town of Coleman was laid out and a rough courthouse built to house the county government and a number of bachelors who had been living out of doors. The present courthouse dates from 1884. When the move began for a new building there was sufficient resistance to prevent demolition. The result was an extensive enlargement and remodeling which cost $190,000 in 1951.

COLLIN COUNTY, MCKINNEY. Collin McKinney was born in New Jersey. He lived in Virginia and Kentucky before settling in Arkansas, six miles from present Texarkana, in 1824. He moved into Bowie County, Texas in 1831, and was the oldest signer of the Declaration of Independence. He was a member of the Congress of the Republic, although there was uncertainty about whether his part of Bowie County was in Texas or Arkansas.

Settlement began in 1842 and Collin County was organized four years later with Buckner the county seat. In 1848 a one-room courthouse was built at McKinney. A two-story frame courthouse, erected in the middle fifties, was replaced in 1874 by the present building, which cost $26,000.

COLLINGSWORTH COUNTY, WELLINGTON. James Collinsworth, of Tennessee, was a member of the Convention of 1836 and an aide to General Sam Houston. He was sent to the United States to explore annexation possibilities in 1836, then was a senator of the Republic and chief justice of the Supreme Court. In 1838, while a candidate for the presidency, he killed himself. The legislature misspelled his name, adding a "g," as they created the county in 1876.

The county remained cattle country for many years. The Rocking Chair Ranch was sold to English investors, which resulted in the Rocking Chair Ranche Company, Limited, whose principal owner was Sir Dudley Coutts Majoribanks, the first Baron of Tweedmouth. Their hands were referred to as "cow servants" and locally the Rocking Chair was called the "nobility ranch." The county was organized in 1890. Wellington was selected over Pearl to be the county seat. Wellington was named for the victor at Waterloo. The first courthouse was begun in 1891. Lumber, nails, and cement had to be brought from Quanah by freight wagon, four or five days away in good weather. The bricks were baked there in Collingsworth County. The $31,000 building was completed in 1893. The second courthouse was built in 1931 for some $150,000 and is still in use.

COLORADO COUNTY, COLUMBUS. The county is named for the Colorado River. Colorado means red, although it is probable that the Colorado River has always been clear and that Spanish explorers mixed up the names of this river and the Brazos, which did run red. Columbus, the county seat, was settled in 1823 by Austin colonists: old Spanish maps call the site Montezuma, indicating that an Indian village was situated there. As he retreated before Santa Anna in March, 1836, Houston had Columbus burned.

Colorado County was one of the original counties of the Republic, organized in 1837. Four courthouses preceded the present one, which was completed in 1891 at a cost of $54,596 plus $1,050 for the clock and $4,615 for jail cells. A hurricane damaged the tower in 1909: the present dome took its place. Some remodeling was done in 1939, and the dome was covered with copper sheathing in 1965.

COMAL COUNTY, NEW BRAUNFELS. The county was named for the Comal River. In Spanish a comal was a flat, earthenware pan for maize cakes, which perhaps resembled the islands in the river or the valley through which it flowed.

New Braunfels, established by German immigrants the year before, became the seat of government on creation of the county in 1846. Temporary facilities were used for keeping records and holding court until the first courthouse was erected in 1860. The present native stone capitol was built in 1898 and cost $36,900. One hundred thousand dollars worth of additions and renovations have since been made.

COMANCHE COUNTY, COMANCHE. Comanche County, created in 1856 from parts of Bosque and Coryell counties, was named by historian and Indian fighter John Henry Brown in honor of the Lords of the Plains. Settlement had begun in 1854. Troy, the first county seat, changed its name to Cora after finding there was already a Troy, Texas.

The first courthouse, in 1856, was a one-room log cabin. After Comanche County territory was included in the new Hamilton County, Cora was no longer near the center of the county. The new county seat town which resulted was Comanche. The courthouse, of stockade or picket construction, burned in 1862. The county rented space until 1875 when a $12,000 two-story, red brick courthouse was completed. In 1890, a three-story, $65,000 structure was built, which was used until 1939. The present $195,000 courthouse was dedicated July 4, 1941.

CONCHO COUNTY, PAINT ROCK. Spaniards came into the county as early as 1650 because of stories of pearls found in the Concho River. Concho means shell. Created in 1858, Concho County was not organized until 1879. Even then the population remained small. Paint Rock is so named because of Indian pictographs located nearby. The first courthouse was a $500 wooden building. The present $40,000 structure was built in 1883.

COOKE COUNTY, GAINESVILLE. William G. Cooke, a Virginian, took part in the siege of Bexar. Later he was quartermaster general of the Republic. He was imprisoned in Mexico because of participation in the Santa Fe Expedition. After his release he married José Navarro's niece.

Edmund Pendleton Gaines, after whom Gainesville was named, was a United States Army captain in 1807 when he arrested Aaron Burr and testified at Burr's treason trial. As a brigadier general he took part in the Black Hawk war. At Stephen Austin's request, he brought American troops to Nacogdoches in July, 1836.

Cooke County was organized in 1848. Two courthouses preceded the present one, built in 1911 at a cost of $125,000.

CORYELL COUNTY, GATESVILLE. James Coryell, of Ohio, hunted for silver in the San Saba country with James and Rezin Bowie. Before the revolution he explored part of present Coryell County. He was a member of Sterling Robertson's ranging company in 1836. Near the falls of the Brazos, Coryell and two companions were raiding a bee tree when Indians killed them.

Gatesville, five miles from Fort Gates, became the county seat upon Coryell County's organization in 1854. At least two courthouses preceded the present $75,000 edifice erected in 1897. The 1872 building cost $12,130.

COTTLE COUNTY, PADUCAH. Tennessean George Washington Cottle was at Gonzales when Travis' request for assistance arrived. Cottle was one of the Gonzales volunteers who entered the Alamo on March 1. He died with the other defenders on March 6, 1836. Cottle County was open range, grazed by cattle from the SMS and Matador ranches for several years after its creation in 1876. There were 24 residents in 1880 and 240 in 1890. Organization was effected in 1892 with Paducah the county seat. The present courthouse was occupied in 1930. It cost $150,000 and was Cottle County's second.

CRANE COUNTY, CRANE. William Carey Crane, a Virginian and graduate of George Washington University, was a Baptist preacher and president of Baylor University from 1863 to 1885. He was a leader in the promotion of the

Texas public school system. Crane County was created in 1887, but twenty years later there were no roads and only 14 people living there. After oil was discovered, the county was organized, in 1927, with Crane the county seat. Crane County's second courthouse was built in 1948. Its original cost was $150,000. In 1958 some $370,000 was spent enlarging and remodeling it.

CROCKETT COUNTY, OZONA. David Crockett was a legend long before he came to Texas. Born in 1786 he roamed the Tennessee countryside as a boy. At 20 he was a private in the army commanded by Andrew Jackson which responded to the Indian attack on Fort Mims. Crockett was a mighty hunter and claimed he killed 105 bears in less than a year. He was a militia colonel and a legislator. When he was defeated for re-election to Congress, he came to Texas, joined Travis and Bowie at the Alamo, and died there.

Crockett County was organized in 1891. In the county seat election the only town, Emerald, was rejected in favor of the site of E. M. Powell's well, which became Ozona. The present courthouse, Crockett County's second, cost $30,000 in 1902.

CROSBY COUNTY, CROSBYTON. Stephen Crosby came to Texas from South Carolina in 1845 and was chief clerk in the Texas Land Office until 1867.

Crosby County was mainly cattle country after the Comanches withdrew to the reservation. In 1879 Paris Cox brought some Quakers into the county: they were the first farmers on the Staked Plains. Their settlement, Estacado, became the county seat in 1886 and Crosbyton became the county seat in 1912. The present $38,000 courthouse, Crosby County's third, was constructed in 1914.

CULBERSON COUNTY, VAN HORN. David B. Culberson came to Texas in 1856. After unsuccessfully opposing secession he became an army officer. Later he served ten terms in the United States Congress. His son, Charles A. Culberson, was governor of Texas and, for 24 years, a United States Senator.

Settlement was slight until the Texas and Pacific reached the county in 1882. Culberson County was organized in 1912, and a $75,000 courthouse was erected at Van Horn that year.

DALLAM COUNTY, DALHART. James Wilmer Dallam, a graduate of Brown University, moved to Matagorda in 1839. His digest of the Texas laws was published in 1845. It was revised and kept current for some 60 years. In his last years he published a newspaper at Matagorda.

Most of Dallam County was in the 3 million acre tract the state used in 1882 to pay for the capitol building. The XIT Ranch was established to utilize that land.

Dallam County was organized in 1891. Texline was succeeded as county seat by Dalhart in 1893. The population was only 146 in 1900, but then the big ranches started selling off land to farmers. Dalhart, in Dallam and Hartley counties, was first called Twist, then Twist Junction, then Denrock—for the Fort Worth and Denver City Railroad and the Chicago, Rock Island and Pacific—but postal officials frowned on Denrock. The first syllables of Dallam and Hartley were then combined for Dalhart.

The first courthouse was at Texline. The next was in old Dalhart, north of the tracks. The existing $200,000 courthouse was built in 1922.

DALLAS COUNTY, DALLAS. According to Herbert Gambrell, Dallas was named for George Mifflin Dallas, the vice president of the United States at annexation, or his brother, Commodore A. J. Dallas, or their father, James Madison's Secretary of the Treasury Alexander James Dallas, or Joseph Dallas, an early Dallas County settler, or the Dallas brothers, James, Walter, and Alexander, who served in the Texas Army.

Dallas County was organized in 1846. Dallas defeated Hord's Ridge and Cedar Springs to be the county seat. A wooden building measuring sixteen feet square, was erected while Dallas was the temporary capital. Then a 16 foot by 32 foot courthouse was erected when Dallas became the permanent seat of government. A brick courthouse in use at the time of the great fire of 1860 came through unscathed. After the railroads reached Dallas a $75,000 courthouse was built in 1873. The 1880 red brick capitol has recently been renovated. It, the Criminal Courts Building (1914), the Records Building (1928), and the Records Building Annex (1954) are dwarfed by the $13.6 million courthouse occupied in 1966.

DAWSON COUNTY, LAMESA. Nicholas Mosby Dawson, a San Jacinto veteran, in 1842 took a company to engage Mexican General Adrian Woll, who had captured San Antonio. Dawson, intending to reinforce Mathew Caldwell's company, found that the Battle of Salado was in progress. He and his 53 men took cover after the Mexicans discovered them. Half his men had been killed when Dawson tried to surrender the rest. After some of the Texans had laid down their arms firing began again. Dawson and thirty-five of his men were killed. Three escaped and of the others only nine lived through their captivity in Perote Prison.

Dawson County was organized in 1905. Lamesa won the county seat election from Chicago, whereupon the Chicagoans moved to Lamesa. The present courthouse, built in 1916, was remodeled and expanded in 1952-1953 at a cost of $275,000.

DEAF SMITH COUNTY, HEREFORD. Erastus "Deaf" Smith, was born in New York. His health was bad when he came to Texas in 1821 but within a few years he was well, except for his deafness. He acquired an extensive knowledge of Texas in his wanderings. When Mexican soldiers kept him from entering San Antonio to see his family, he joined the Texan Army and was at the battles of Concepción and San Jacinto.

When Deaf Smith County was organized in 1890 the 97 voters chose Grenada to be the county seat over Ayr. Both were sites only: Ayr's improvements never were more than a single dugout. Since there was already a Grenada, Texas, the county seat became La Plata. In 1891 a $41,000 two-story frame courthouse was built there. But the railroad missed La Plata and in 1898 Hereford became the county seat. The courthouse and the other La Plata buildings were moved to Hereford. The present marble courthouse, erected in 1910 at a cost of $125,000, was given a $354,000 remodeling in 1960-1961.

DELTA COUNTY, COOPER. Delta County, one of the smaller Texas counties, was named for the delta shape of its eastern portion, a triangle formed by the confluence of the North and South Sulphur rivers.

Cooper was named for state Senator L. W. Cooper, who assisted in the county's creation. Delta County was organized in 1870 with Cooper the county seat. The third courthouse, built in 1940-41, presently serves Delta County.

DENTON COUNTY, DENTON. John B. Denton, of Tennessee, was an itinerant Methodist minister in Arkansas and Missouri before becoming a Clarksville, Texas, attorney in the late 1830's. He was one of Colonel Edward H. Tarrant's Ranger captains and was killed in the battle of Village Creek east of modern Fort Worth on May 22, 1841. He was reburied on the Denton courthouse square in 1901.

Denton County was created in 1846. Pinckneyville was succeeded by Alton as county seat. But Alton had a water problem, so the legislature permitted removal of the county seat and the name Alton to a location 5 miles below modern Denton. There the first courthouse, of logs, was built. In 1856, the town and county seat moved again and changed its name to Denton. The frame courthouse, built north of the square in 1857, burned in 1875. Then a two-story brick was erected on the square in 1876: it cost $40,000, but by 1894 it was condemned and razed. The present courthouse was completed in 1896 at a cost of $147,000.

DEWITT COUNTY, CUERO. Kentuckian Green C. DeWitt was a Missouri sheriff before he obtained an empresario grant to bring 400 families to Texas. Settlement began in 1825. The capital of his colony was Gonzales.

DeWitt County was formed from parts of Gonzales, Goliad, and Victoria counties. Upon organization in 1846 Cameron was the county seat, but in the next four years county government moved four times amid a flurry of lawsuits and elections. Clinton was the capital from 1850 until 1876, when the county seat was established at Cuero, an old town whose Spanish name meant "hides." The present $95,000 courthouse was constructed in 1897. Remodeling, sixty years later, cost the county $565,000.

DICKENS COUNTY, DICKENS. Dickens County was named for J. Dickens, one of the Alamo defenders. The county was created in 1876. The first settlement consisted of dugouts used as line camps for ranches such as the Spur, the Pitchfork, and the Matador. The 1880 population was 28, all cowhands. Organization came in 1891. Dickens was the county seat. Temporary facilities were used until the 1893 courthouse was built. It cost $25,000 and was remodeled in 1936.

DIMMITT COUNTY, CARRIZO SPRINGS. Phillip Dimmitt, a Kentuckian, came to Texas in 1822. He ran a trading post east of Lavaca Bay and in October, 1835 was with George Collinsworth and others when they seized Goliad. Dimmitt took part in the siege of Bexar and was at the Alamo until February 23, 1836. On July 4, 1841, Dimmitt and three others were seized at Corpus Christi by Mexican soldiers and marched toward Mexico City. Some of the prisoners escaped at Saltillo: apparently Dimmitt killed himself upon learning he would be executed if the escapees did not return.

John Townsend, a Negro from Nacogdoches, attempted an early settlement, but was driven out by Indians. The first permanent settlement was made in 1865.

Dimmitt County was organized in 1880 with the county seat at Carrizo Springs.

Carrizo is Spanish for cane, referring to reeds growing at the springs for which the town was named. The courthouse, occupied in 1884, cost $14,000. It was remodeled in 1926.

DONLEY COUNTY, CLARENDON. Stockton P. Donley, born in Missouri, attended Transylvania University and began practicing law at Rusk, Texas, in 1847. He was a Confederate officer and was elected to the Texas Supreme Court in 1866. General Sheridan removed him as an impediment to Reconstruction.

The county was first organized in 1876 as Wegefarth County, but in 1882 Donley County took its present form. Clarendon, the capital, was named for Lewis Carhart's wife, Clara. Carhart, a Methodist minister, had founded the town intending that it be devoted to religion and temperance. Cowhands scoffed at these ambitions and called Clarendon "the Saints' Roost," and a panhandle judge sentenced a man to 30 days in Clarendon, which he considered the punishment most approximating solitary confinement. The first courthouse, erected in 1894, still serves Donley County.

DUVAL COUNTY, SAN DIEGO. Duval County was named after Burr, John, and Thomas Duval, sons of William Pope Duval. Burr organized the Kentucky Mustangs to fight in the revolution. He joined Fannin and died in the Goliad Massacre, Palm Sunday, 1836. John Duval, a member of his brother's company, escaped the massacre. He was a Ranger and Confederate soldier and wrote *The Adventures of Big Foot Wallace* and other works. J. Frank Dobie called him the first Texas man of letters. Thomas Duval held several state offices and was a federal judge in Texas before and after the Civil War.

Duval County was organized in 1876. San Diego was the capital. A two-story stone building was rented for $400 a year until a $3,700, two-story frame courthouse was finished in 1879. It burned in 1914 under suspicious circumstances. The present building was erected in 1916 at a cost of $70,000. An annex was built in 1938.

EASTLAND COUNTY, EASTLAND. Kentuckian William Mosby Eastland settled near La Grange and was in the Battle of San Jacinto. For awhile he was a Ranger captain. He participated in the Somervell Expedition and the attack on Mier. He was one of the unfortunates who drew black beans and was shot at Hacienda Salado by order of Santa Anna on March 25, 1843.

Eastland County was created in 1858. The 1860 census showed a population of 99. The county was organized in 1873. Merriman, the county seat, was simply the headquarters buildings of Flannegan's Ranch. In 1875 the county government was moved to Eastland. The present courthouse, Eastland County's fourth, cost $313,000 in 1928.

ECTOR COUNTY, ODESSA. Mathew Duncan Ector was a Georgia legislator before he moved to Henderson in 1850. He rose from private to brigadier general in the Confederate Army. He was one of the district judges removed by General Sheridan as impediments to Reconstruction. Later he was the first presiding judge of the Court of Appeals.

Ector County was organized in 1891: a year earlier the population was 224. A railroad official thought the country resembled the steppes of Russia and named Odessa accordingly. The first courthouse was a sanitarium that had been moved onto the square. A courthouse built in 1904 was replaced in 1938 by a $245,000 model which was enlarged and remodeled in 1964 at a cost of $1.5 million.

EDWARDS COUNTY, ROCKSPRINGS. Haden Edwards was the empresario whose problems precipitated the Fredonian Rebellion. He was a Virginian, and he had obtained a grant in 1825 to locate 800 families in East Texas. Settlers already living in the area assigned to him refused to recognize his authority over their land and the resulting conflicts caused Edwards trouble with the Mexican authorities. While he was away seeking financial support in May, 1826, his brother, Benjamin Edwards, declared the independence of the Nacogdoches area, calling it the Republic of Fredonia. Texas militia and Mexican troops in January, 1827 chased the Fredonians across the Sabine. Haden Edwards gave up his colonization enterprise.

Indian troubles continued into 1879, when Nick Coalson's family was massacred. Edwards County was organized in 1883. Bullhead won the county seat election from Leakey. Bullhead became Vance, and another election moved the government to Leakey. In 1891, Rocksprings became the county seat with the Wallace and Stewart store housing county operations temporarily. The present courthouse cost $18,000 and was finished in 1891. An 1897 fire destroyed many of the early records and damaged the building. In 1927 a tornado took the roof off.

ELLIS COUNTY, WAXAHACHIE. Ellis County was probably named for Virginian Richard Ellis, who was an Alabama Supreme Court justice before coming to Texas. He was president of the 1836 convention and a senator of the Republic.

The county was organized in 1850 with Waxahachie the county seat. Waxahachie is an Indian word meaning cow creek or buffalo creek. The first courthouse was built in 1850 at a cost of $59. The second, a two-story edifice, cost $1,999 in 1854. The third, twenty years later, ran $40,000, and the present courthouse, completed in 1896, cost $175,000.

EL PASO COUNTY, EL PASO. Settlement has existed at El Paso del Norte, The Pass of the North, since Cabeza de Vaca was there four and a third centuries ago. The oldest Texas settlement, Ysleta, dates from the 1680's.

Santa Fe County, formed in 1848, included present El Paso County, which was created in 1850. The first county seat was San Elizario, then Ysleta from 1866 to 1868. San Elizario was the capital again from 1868 to 1873 when Ysleta once more prevailed. In 1881 the railroads reached El Paso, generating activity and growth. El Paso became the county seat in 1883. The first courthouse was at San Elizario and the second at Ysleta. The fourth courthouse burned in 1916, and the present one was built the next year, costing $1 million for building and furnishings. Some $3.5 million worth of remodeling and additions were made in the late 1950's. The courthouse accommodates city, as well as county, offices.

ERATH COUNTY, STEPHENVILLE. George Bernard Erath, born in Vienna, Austria, reached Texas in 1833. He was a Ranger and surveyor and fought at San Jacinto. Although he was a member of the Somervell Expedition, he did not go on to Mier, where the others were captured. He served in the Texas Congress and the legislature, laid out Caldwell and Waco, and was a Confederate officer. Erath County settlement began in 1854 with the arrival of John and William Stephen, who founded Stephenville. The county was organized in 1856 with Stephenville the county seat. The third courthouse still serves the county. It cost $75,000 in 1892 and was renovated in 1950.

FALLS COUNTY, MARLIN. Settlement began prior to the revolution, but Falls County was abandoned during the Runaway Scrape. John Marlin's family was the first to return after San Jacinto. They settled at Bucksnort. The falls of the Brazos River was an early landmark. Falls County was created out of Milam and Limestone counties. It was organized in 1850 with Old Viesca the first county seat, but almost immediately Adams, which became Marlin, succeeded Old Viesca. The present courthouse is Falls County's fourth—fire destroyed one in the 1870's—and it cost $219,000 in 1939.

FANNIN COUNTY, BONHAM. The names Fannin and Bonham make an interesting combination. James Butler Bonham, a South Carolina schoolmate of William Barret Travis, was twice sent from the Alamo to get help. The first time he asked Fannin's aid. After returning to the Alamo, he went to Goliad and Gonzales and had to ride through Mexican troops on March 3, to re-enter the Alamo, where he died three days later. James Walker Fannin, Jr. of Georgia, attended West Point for awhile and settled at Velasco in 1834. Fannin was about to descend on Matamoras when he learned it was well garrisoned and fell back to Goliad. After failing to respond to Travis' call his actions were indecisive and finally he surrendered. Most of his men were killed at the Goliad Massacre, March 27, 1836. Fannin had been wounded previously, and he was taken from the hospital and shot.

Fannin County was organized in 1838 with Tulip or Lexington the first county seat. County business was transacted at Jacob Black's cabin. A log courthouse was built at Old Warren in 1840. The county seat was moved to Bois d'Arc, which became Bonham, in 1843. The first Bonham courthouse was a one-room log house which became a dog trot with the addition of another cabin and connecting breezeway. In 1881, a brick building, with a white fence, was erected, succeeded in 1888 by a native stone courthouse having clocks on four sides of the tower. A fire in 1929 caused the building to be renovated. A $500,000 remodeling was completed in 1966.

FAYETTE COUNTY, LA GRANGE. Fayette County was within the first Austin grant and was a prospective site for the capital of the Republic. Houston vetoed the bill locating the capital there.

Fayette County was an original county of the Republic. Organized in 1838, it was named for the Marquis de Lafayette. Early settlers from La Grange, Fayette County, Tennessee, were responsible for naming the new county seat La Grange. Three courthouses preceded the present one, built in 1891 for $87,356.

FISHER COUNTY, ROBY. Samuel Rhoads Fisher, of Pennsylvania, settled at Matagorda in 1830. He signed the Texas Declaration of Independence and was Houston's secretary of the navy.

The 1880 Fisher County population was 136, only four of whom were farmers. The others ranched. The county was organized in 1886. Roby was the county seat. One courthouse preceded the present $65,000 structure built in 1910. The dome was removed when it was remodeled in 1951.

FLOYD COUNTY, FLOYDADA. Dolphin Ward Floyd, one of the Gonzales volunteers who responded to **William Barret Travis'** call, died at the Alamo March 6, 1836.

Floyd County settlement began in 1884. Upon organization, in 1890, Della Plain, Floyd City, and Lockney were prospective county seat locations. When it was apparent they could not win, the Lockney people helped choose Floyd City, 55 votes to 33. Floyd City became Floydada. The second courthouse burned in 1948. The present one was built in 1950 and cost $275,000.

FOARD COUNTY, CROWELL. Robert J. Foard was a Marylander and Princeton graduate who practiced law at Columbus, Texas. He was a Confederate Army major. His law partner, a state senator when the county was created, suggested it be named for him.

In December, 1860, a ranging party led by Sul Ross and which included Charles Goodnight recovered Cynthia Ann Parker nine miles north of present Crowell. She had been captured by Comanches when she was a child, in 1836.

Foard County was organized in 1891 with Crowell the county seat. One courthouse preceded the existing $60,000 building of 1910 vintage.

FORT BEND COUNTY, RICHMOND. Fort Bend was an outpost built in 1821 at the bend of the Brazos River. In 1836, Santa Anna crossed there as he pursued Houston's retreating army to San Jacinto.

Fort Bend was carved out of Austin County and was organized in 1838. Richmond, at the site of the old fort, became the county seat. The present courthouse, erected in 1908, is the third for the county. Its original cost was $66,050. **Remodeling in 1940 and 1958 cost $40,000 and $115,928 respectively.**

FRANKLIN COUNTY, MOUNT VERNON. Benjamin Cromwell Franklin, a Georgian, fought at San Jacinto and was the first judge appointed during the Republic.

Settlement began in 1836. Franklin County was created from Titus County and organized in 1875. The first commissioners court changed the name of the county seat, Lone Star, to commemorate George Washington's estate. The present $42,000 courthouse is the county's second and was occupied in 1912.

FREESTONE COUNTY, FAIRFIELD. Eastern Limestone County became Freestone County in 1850 and was organized the next year. Mount Pleasant, the county seat, was renamed by former residents of Fairfield, Alabama. Temporary facilities were used until a frame courthouse was erected in 1855. A two-story brick structure replaced the frame building in 1891. The existing courthouse was finished in 1919 and cost $136,000.

FRIO COUNTY, PEARSALL. Frio County—frio means cold—was named after the Frio River. La Salle passed through the county in 1685, as did the Spaniards searching for him.

The county was created in 1858, but since ranching was the main occupation, the 1870 census reported only 309 residents. It was organized in 1871. Frio Town was founded at the Presidio crossing of the Frio River to serve as the county seat. A stone courthouse was built there in 1876. When the railroad missed Frio Town, the new town of Pearsall, on the right of way, became the county seat in 1883. Most of Frio Town's frame buildings were dismantled and rebuilt at Pearsall. The 1904 Frio County courthouse, which cost $30,000, is the fourth.

GAINES COUNTY, SEMINOLE. James Gaines, a Virginian born in 1776, was a member of the Gutiérrez-Magee expedition in 1813. He was alcalde of the Sabine district in the 1820's and opposed the Fredonian Rebellion. A signer of the Texas Declaration of Independence, he was a congressman of the Republic. He followed the gold rush and died in California in 1856.

Gaines County was organized in 1905, twenty-nine years after its creation. Its population was 8 in 1880 and 55 in 1900. Three courthouses preceded the present $75,000 edifice built at Seminole in 1955.

GALVESTON COUNTY, GALVESTON. Bernardo de Gálvez was the Spanish governor of Louisiana from 1777 to 1783 and aided the Americans during the revolution. He captured Florida, Jamaica, and the Bahamas from the British, for which the king made him a general and a count. He ordered the Texas coast surveyed, and the surveyors named Galveston Bay for him. In 1785, he succeeded his father as Mexican viceroy.

The history of Galveston Island goes back to Cabeza de Vaca. Those who sojourned there included the pirate Jean Lafitte and the ad interim government of the Republic of Texas, which sought to evade Santa Anna. Galveston County was organized in 1838. Its county seat, Galveston, was Texas' largest city. The present courthouse, constructed in 1966 at a cost of some $2.5 million, is the third and replaced an 1898 building.

GARZA COUNTY, POST. Garza County was buffalo country when it was created in 1876. Four years later there were 36 residents. The last Indian raid occurred in 1883, but the population was down to 14 because of drought in 1890. In another decade, after wells had been drilled to minimize the water problem, there were 180 Garza County residents. Garza County was named for a pioneer family. It was organized in 1907.

Post City, the county seat, was founded by Charles W. Post, who had made a fortune on Postum, Grape Nuts, and Elijah's Manna (which became Post Toasties). Post developed the town as a colonization experiment. A tent was used prior to completion of a small rock courthouse in 1908. The present seat of justice cost $8,000 in 1923.

GILLESPIE COUNTY, FREDERICKSBURG. Kentucky-born Richard Addison Gillespie opened a store in Texas in 1837, fought Indians, and was a member of the Somervell Expedition. He was wounded in Ranger service, and in 1846 was killed at Monterrey during the Mexican War.

Gillespie County was settled by Germans in 1846. Fredericksburg was named for Prince Frederick of Prussia, a supporter of the Adelsverein, which sponsored

German settlement of New Braunfels and Fredericksburg. The county was organized in 1848 with Fredericksburg the capital. Two courthouses preceded the present one, which was occupied in 1939 and cost $120,000.

GLASSCOCK COUNTY, GARDEN CITY. In 1832 George Washington Glasscock had a partnership with another Kentuckian, Abraham Lincoln, operating a flatboat on Illinois' Sangamon River. He was in the siege of Bexar, and Georgetown, Williamson County, was named for him, since he donated the 172-acre townsite.

Glasscock County was organized in 1893. Max Greenwood, in the *Handbook of Texas*, said, "There has never been a saloon or a beer joint in Glasscock County. In 1944, there was no newspaper, no railroad, no bank, no health officer, no lawyer and no doctor. For a period of seven consecutive years the jail was never used. Two paved highways make motor transportation possible. Population was 1,090 in 1950." There were 1,137 residents in 1970.

The county seat was originally New California, then Dixie, which changed its name to Garden City. The second courthouse was finished in 1909 and cost $28,000.

GOLIAD COUNTY, GOLIAD. The Goliad townsite was occupied by an Indian village in 1749 when the Mission Nuestra Señora del Espirito Santo de Zuñiga and the Presidio Nuestra Señora de Loreto were relocated there. The mission, the presidio, and the settlement that grew up around them were called La Bahía.

In 1829 the Congress of Coahuila y Texas changed the name of La Bahía to Goliad, an anagram of Hidalgo. Father Miguel Hidalgo y Costilla had been executed for his leadership of an unsuccessful revolt against the Spaniards.

Goliad County was created in 1836 and organized in 1837. The second courthouse, built in 1870, burned, and was replaced by the present $65,000 building, erected in 1889.

GONZALES COUNTY, GONZALES. Rafael Gonzales, born in Bexar in 1789, was an officer in the Spanish Army. He joined the independence movement and became a Mexican Army officer. He was governor of the state of Coahuila y Texas when the DeWitt colony was established.

Gonzales County was in the heart of Green DeWitt's colony. The Texas Revolution began there in October, 1836. It was one of the original counties of the Republic, organized in 1837 with Gonzales the county seat. The present Gonzales courthouse was occupied in 1896. Its cost was $54,500. Two others preceded it.

GRAY COUNTY, PAMPA. Virginian Peter W. Gray came to Texas in 1838. He was an Indian fighter and second lieutenant in the Milam Guards when they moved to repel a Mexican invasion. He was a district attorney, legislator, district judge, and Confederate congressman. Later he was a Texas Supreme Court justice.

Lefors was the county seat when Gray County was organized in 1902. Pampa—the Spanish word for plains is pampa—became the county seat in 1928 and the present courthouse was begun soon thereafter. It cost some $300,000.

GRAYSON COUNTY, SHERMAN. Peter William Grayson, a Kentuckian, began practicing law at San Felipe, the Austin colony capital in 1830. He and Spencer Jack went to Mexico in 1834 to seek Austin's release—the Mexicans had imprisoned Austin when he was in Mexico City to present a petition—and Grayson was Austin's aide during the revolution. He was attorney general under President Burnet and went with James Collinsworth to the United States to obtain recognition for Texas. He was running for president against M. B. Lamar in 1838 when he took his own life, probably because of bad health.

Settlement began in 1836, and Grayson County was cut out of Fannin County in 1846. Sherman was the county seat, honoring Colonel Sidney Sherman who fought in the Battle of San Jacinto. The county has had five courthouses. The fourth burned. The present one was completed in 1936 at a cost of $306,000. A wing added in the late 1960's cost some $410,000.

GREGG COUNTY, LONGVIEW. John Gregg moved to Fairfield, Texas from Alabama in 1854. He was a state judge and a member of the Secession Convention and the Provisional Congress of the Confederacy. He was captured at Fort Donelson. After his exchange he was promoted to brigadier general and was killed in 1864 commanding Hood's Texas Brigade.

Gregg County was formed from Upshur, Rusk, and Harrison counties and was organized in 1873 with Longview the county seat. The first courthouse was an existing building presented to the county by a citizens committee. The sheriff was ordered to make the building free of leaks, but it was impossible. The county clerk complained that records could not be kept there safely, the walls were a single layer of planks through which the rain came, and anyone who wished could kick his way inside. The commissioners rented space for county use until a $13,000 courthouse was ready for occupancy in 1879. A two-story brick, in 1897, succeeded the old building, which had been condemned: the contractor agreed to build the new courthouse and tear down the old one for $27,450. The present five-story courthouse was begun in 1932. The contract price was $194,500. A $607,000 annex was constructed in 1958.

GRIMES COUNTY, ANDERSON. Jesse Grimes, born in North Carolina, settled in present Grimes County in 1827. He was an officer of the municipality, then a member of the 1835 Consultation, and a signer of the Declaration of Independence. He served in the senates of the Republic and state.

Austin's colonists began settling in the county in 1821. Grimes County was organized in 1846, having been created from Montgomery County. Two courthouses preceded the present one at Anderson, which was built in 1893, cost $12,597, and is a little jewel.

GUADALUPE COUNTY, SEGUIN. Captain Alonso de León named the Guadalupe River for the Lady of Guadalupe portrayed on his standard. The river runs through Guadalupe County.

Guadalupe County was part of the DeWitt colony. It was created in 1846 with Seguin the county seat.

Erasmo Seguin was born at Bexar in 1782. He helped supply the Texas Army throughout the revolution. His son, Juan, was an army officer and was ordered to follow the retreating Mexican Army out of Texas. Then he was to take charge of San Antonio until the civil government could be reorganized. Seguin was named for him in 1839. Later, while he was mayor of Bexar, he was accused of disloyalty to Texas. He left Bexar in 1842 and was a member of the army of Mexican General Adrian Woll that invaded Texas later that year. In 1848, after the Mexican War, he was permitted to return to Texas.

One courthouse existed before the present one was built in 1935 at a cost of $300,000.

HALE COUNTY, PLAINVIEW. John C. Hale, born in Maine, settled in Sabine County in 1831. He was killed at San Jacinto.

The first settler came to Hale County in 1883. Methodist minister Horatio Graves experimented with farming and encouraged immigration. Hale County was organized in 1888. Plainview—where there grew a grove of hackberries said to be the only trees on the plains—was the county seat. Three frame courthouses preceded the present building, erected in 1910. Its $70,651 cost included the jail.

HALL COUNTY, MEMPHIS. Warren D. C. Hall was born in North Carolina and practiced law in Natchitoches. He was a member of the 1812 Gutiérrez-Magee Expedition until Gutiérrez executed some of the prisoners. In 1817, Hall was in Texas with Louis and Michele Aury. He moved to Brazoria County in 1835 and was Burnet's adjutant general and secretary of war of the Republic. In 1842 he was in the band that pursued Mexican General Adrian Woll's invading army.

Hall County's population was 36 in 1880. The railroad arrived in 1887, and the county had 203 residents when it was organized in 1890 with Memphis the county seat. The present courthouse is Hall County's third and cost $150,000 in 1923.

HAMILTON COUNTY, HAMILTON. Governor James Hamilton of South Carolina gave financial help to Texas' provisional government during the revolution. Then President Lamar authorized him to seek a $5 million loan in the United States. He negotiated treaties with England and the Netherlands and helped James Pinckney Henderson make a treaty with France. When Sam Houston became President in 1841 he terminated Hamilton's authority to represent the Republic. In 1857 Hamilton was on his way to collect $210,000 owed him by Texas when his ship sank and he drowned in the Gulf.

The town of Hamilton had its beginnings in 1838, but the county was not organized until 1856. Buildings serving as the Hamilton County capitol burned on three occasions. For the first twenty years county government operated in rented space, stores, a livery stable, a school house, and a saloon. In 1878 an $11,559 native stone structure was built. It burned in 1886. The next courthouse, built in 1886-1887, cost $30,000 and is the center portion of the present county building, which was expanded and remodeled in 1932.

HANSFORD COUNTY, SPEARMAN. John M. Hansford, a Kentucky physician, was speaker of the Texas Congress and district judge. Hansford was killed in East Texas's Regulator-Moderator strife in 1844.

The four English-born Cator brothers were the first white men in the county. They were buffalo hunters. James Cator turned his camp into a trading post in 1875.

In 1889 when organization came, Hansford was chosen over Farwell to be the county seat. The first officials included County Judge James Cator and Sheriff Bert Cator. Spearman became the county seat in 1920 after the Santa Fe railroad arrived. Two courthouses preceded the $49,000 building erected in 1931 that now serves the county.

HARDEMAN COUNTY, QUANAH. Bailey Hardeman and Thomas Hardeman moved to Texas from Tennessee in 1835. Bailey Hardeman helped draft the Declaration of Independence, was one of Burnet's cabinet officers, and signed the Treaty of Velasco. Thomas Hardeman was a congressman during the Republic and later a legislator. In 1850 he was Grand Master of Masons in Texas.

Hardeman County was organized in 1884, the year the first settlements were made. Margaret, the first county seat, was succeeded after a few months by Quanah, a townsite on the railroad. By consent, the residency test for the county seat election was whether a man's laundry had been done in a Hardeman County town for at least six weeks. As a result section hands laying the Fort Worth and Denver track were qualified voters. They favored Quanah, named for the last war chief of the Quahadi Comanches, Quanah Parker. One court-house preceded the present $50,000 building, which was completed in 1908.

HARDIN COUNTY, KOUNTZE. The Hardin brothers, Augustine, Benjamin, Franklin, Milton, and William, came from Georgia by way of Tennessee to settle in present Liberty County. Augustine, in 1827, helped put down the Fredonian Rebellion. Later he signed the Declaration of Independence. Benjamin, the oldest, was under indictment for murder when he came to Texas. He became sheriff of Liberty County and a member of the Texas Congress. Franklin was arrested on extradition proceedings for the killing that had caused the Hardins to leave Tennessee. When Tennessee officers did not come for him, he was released. William, arrested on extradition proceedings, escaped twice. The last time he remained free. He was alcalde of Liberty in 1832 and a delegate to the 1833 convention. Franklin was secretary of the Liberty ayuntamiento in 1831. He was in the siege of Bexar and during the Republic was a militia colonel. He was a member of the 1867 legislature that created Hardin County. Milton, the youngest, died in Johnson County in 1898.

Hardin was the first county seat after organization in 1858. The courthouse burned in 1887 and Kountze became the capital. The fourth Hardin County courthouse was completed in 1959. Its cost was $1.5 million, including furnishings.

HARRIS COUNTY, HOUSTON. New Yorker John Richardson Harris was in Saint Genevieve, Missouri, when Moses Austin talked to him about Texas. In 1824 he settled on Buffalo Bayou in present Harris County. Two years later he had Francis Johnson survey the town of Harrisburg. He died of yellow fever while on a New Orleans business trip in 1829.

Harrisburg was burned by Santa Anna just before the battle of San Jacinto: he had hoped to find the ad interim Texas government there. The Allen brothers founded Houston in 1836 to fill the commercial vacuum created by the destruction of Harrisburg. Houston was the first county seat when Harrisburg County was organized in 1837. The name was shortened to Harris in 1839. Houston has had five courthouses, the first a log cabin. The fourth, erected in 1910, was remodeled in 1953 at a cost of $2.7 million and is now the Civil Courts Building. The present $7.3 million courthouse was built in 1953.

HARRISON COUNTY, MARSHALL. Jonas Harrison of New Jersey was Master in Chancery for New York state before he settled in Shelby County, Texas, in 1820. He was an alcalde of Teneha and a member of the 1832 convention. Harrison was one of the earliest proponents of Texas independence. He died a few months after San Jacinto.

Harrison County was created in 1839. Marshall—for long-time United States Chief Justice John Marshall—was the county seat. Three courthouses preceded the present one, built in 1964 at a cost of $1,208,000. The third still stands, a beautiful building erected in 1900 that has been recently renovated.

HARTLEY COUNTY, CHANNING. Oliver Cromwell Hartley, a Virginian and graduate of Marshall College, began practicing law in Galveston in 1846. His *Digest of the Laws of Texas* was published in 1850. He was the reporter of Supreme Court decisions for many years. The county was named for him and his brother, Rufus K. Hartley.

Hartley County was organized in 1891. Hartley was the first seat of justice. Channing, the XIT Ranch headquarters, won the county seat election in 1903, and XIT cowboys jacked up the frame courthouse and moved it on wheels to Channing. In 1906 the present $14,000 brick courthouse was erected. The frame building became a hotel.

HASKELL COUNTY, HASKELL. Charles Ready Haskell, of Tennessee, was with Burr Duval's company at the battle of Coleto and was among the men Fannin surrendered. He was killed in the Goliad Massacre, March 27, 1836.

Haskell County was organized in 1885. Haskell, the only settlement, became the county seat. An early saloon was The Road to Ruin: for lack of other facilities church services were held there. One courthouse was built in 1885. The existing capitol cost $100,000 in 1906. It was remodeled in 1931.

HAYS COUNTY, SAN MARCOS. Several early settlers were members of John Coffee Hays' Rangers, and they got the county named for him. Jack Hays came to Texas from Tennessee in the 1830's. He was one of the most effective of the Ranger captains. In 1849 he took a caravan west and was San Francisco County sheriff for four years. As California surveyor general he laid out the city of Oakland.

In 1848 Hays County was organized with the seat of government at San Marcos. The 1848 vintage wooden courthouse burned in 1881. A two-story masonry building, erected in 1882, burned in 1908. The present courthouse cost $39,000 in 1908.

HEMPHILL COUNTY, CANADIAN. John Hemphill, of South Carolina, fought in the Seminole wars before coming to Texas and participating in the Council House Fight at San Antonio in 1840. He took part in the campaign against the Rafael Vasquez invasion and was an officer in the Somervell Expedition. He was chief justice of the Texas Supreme Court—a position he had also held under the Republic—until he succeeded Sam Houston as United States senator in 1857. A secessionist, he was a Confederate congressman at his death.

Hemphill County was organized in 1887 with Canadian the county seat. The present courthouse, built in 1909 for $31,278, is the county's second.

HENDERSON COUNTY, ATHENS. James Pinckney Henderson practiced law in North Carolina and Mississippi before coming to Texas. President David G. Burnet made him a brigadier general and sent him to recruit troops in the United States. He was first attorney general and then succeeded Stephen F. Austin as secretary of state of the Republic. Through his efforts, England and France recognized Texas. He was a member of the Convention of 1845. The legislature gave Governor Henderson a leave of absence to command Texas troops in the Mexican War. He succeeded T.J. Rusk as United States senator in 1857 and died in Washington the next year.

After organization in 1846, Buffalo was the county seat, succeeded in 1850 by Athens. The present courthouse, the third, was built in 1913 and cost $113,500.

HIDALGO COUNTY, EDINBURG. Hidalgo County was named for Father Miguel Hidalgo y Costilla, the priest who began a revolution at Dolores, Mexico, in 1810. His forces were defeated and he was shot in 1811, but his insurrection is usually cited as the beginning of Mexico's independence movement.

There were attempts at colonization in the 18th century, but settlement really dates from La Habitacion, established about 1850 across the Rio Grande from Reynosa. A Scot, John Young, changed the name to Edinburg and it became the first county seat. In 1908 the town's name was changed to Hidalgo, and Chapin, fourteen miles away, became Edinburg and the county seat.

Hidalgo County was organized in 1852. Four courthouses preceded the $1.5 million building erected in 1954.

HILL COUNTY, HILLSBORO. Hill County, organized in 1853, was named for George Washington Hill, a Tennessee surgeon who came to Texas in 1836. He was a member of the Texas Congress and secretary of war and navy under Presidents Houston and Jones.

Citizens were to select a county seat location which was to be named Hillsborough. Until then, county business was to be transacted at Lexington. After using a log building temporarily a $200 frame courthouse was erected in 1853. It was succeeded by a two-story brick which burned in 1872. Another two-story brick, costing $15,000, was finished in 1878. The present $83,000 capitol building was occupied in 1890.

HOCKLEY COUNTY, LEVELLAND. Philadelphian George W. Hockley met Sam Houston in Washington. He moved to Tennessee when Houston became governor in 1828. Seven years later he came to Texas. During the revolution he was Houston's chief of staff and was secretary of war in both Houston administrations. He accompanied Santa Anna to Washington.

Hockley County was organized in 1921, nearly half a century after its creation. It had 137 residents. Ropesville contended against Hockley City, an uninhabited tract, for the courthouse and lost. The commissioners felt they should hold their initial meeting on the courthouse square, but they could not even find Hockley City because the surveyor's markers had been knocked down by cattle. A cowhand located the site and the commissioners held their meeting there in a Cadillac automobile. Hockley City was renamed Levelland in 1922. A wooden building served until 1928 when the present $100,000 courthouse was constructed.

HOOD COUNTY, GRANBURY. General John Bell Hood, of Kentucky, graduated from West Point in 1853. He resigned his commission in April 1861, to join the Confederate Army. As a major general, he lost an arm at Gettysburg and his right leg at Chickamauga. In 1864 he was promoted to lieutenant general. He died in New Orleans in 1879.

Hood County was organized in 1866. Three elections and the service of arbitrators were required to select a county seat: Granbury, honoring General Hiram Bronson Granberry—Hood County does not spell the name the way the general did—the commander of Hood's Texas Brigade, who was killed in Franklin, Tennessee in late 1864. The first courthouse was burned in 1875. The existing 1890 building was remodeled in 1959 and its tower was repaired in 1970.

HOPKINS COUNTY, SULPHUR SPRINGS. Indiana-born David Hopkins came to present Hopkins County when he was a boy, not long after the first settlement was made in 1842. The county was created from Lamar and Nacogdoches in 1846. Tarrant was the capital. After Rains and Delta counties were carved from its territory in 1870 and part of Lamar County was added, Sulphur Springs became the county seat in 1871. The present courthouse, Hopkins County's third, was built in 1894 for $40,000.

HOUSTON COUNTY, CROCKETT. Sam Houston was was born March 2, 1793 near Lexington, Virginia. After his father's death the family moved to Maryville, Tennessee. As a boy Houston lived with the Cherokees for three years. In 1814 he attracted General Andrew Jackson's attention. He became congressman, then governor of Tennessee. Because of marital difficulties he resigned as governor and lived for several years with the Cherokees in the Indian Territory, present Oklahoma. Houston represented Nacogdoches at the 1833 convention, was delegate to the 1835 Consultation, commanded Texas troops, and was the victor at San Jacinto. He was twice president of the Republic, and he and T. J. Rusk were Texas' first United States senators. He was governor at the time of secession: when he refused to swear allegiance to the Confederacy he was removed from office.

Houston County was created in 1837. The donor of the county seat townsite required that it be named for David Crockett, killed at the Alamo the previous year. The existing courthouse, which cost $400,000 in 1939, is Houston County's third.

HOWARD COUNTY, BIG SPRING. Volney Erskine Howard, of Maine, was a Mississippi legislator and published the Vicksburg Mississipian before moving to San Antonio. He served in the 1845 constitutional convention, the first Texas legislature, and the United States Congress. Later he practiced law in San Francisco, Sacramento, and Los Angeles and was a delegate to the California constitutional convention.

Settlement came late to Howard County. One of the early residents was the Earl of Aylesford, an English nobleman who, in 1883, ranched 37,000 acres. Howard County was organized in 1882. The county seat was Big Spring, a collection of buffalo hunters' hide huts and saloons. Three courthouses preceded the present one, built in 1953 for $850,000.

HUDSPETH COUNTY, SIERRA BLANCA. Claude Benton Hudspeth, a peace officer and newspaper editor, represented El Paso in the legislature and United States Congress for 29 years.

Hudspeth, created from El Paso County in 1917, is the second largest county. The present courthouse, begun in 1919 and finished in 1921 at a cost of approximately $35,000, is the only one the county has had.

HUNT COUNTY, GREENVILLE. Memucan Hunt was born in North Carolina, moved to Mississippi in 1834, and reached Texas soon after San Jacinto. Anticipating a Mexican invasion, President Burnet made him a brigadier general in August, 1836. Houston sent Hunt to obtain American recognition and he became the Texan minister to Washington. He was Lamar's secretary of the navy and served in the army during the Mexican War.

Hunt County was taken from Fannin and Nacogdoches counties in 1846. The present $400,000 courthouse was completed in 1929 and is Hunt County's seventh.

HUTCHINSON COUNTY, STINNETT. Anderson Hutchinson, a Virginian, practiced law in Tennessee, Alabama, Mississippi, and Texas. He was the presiding judge in the case resulting from the chastising, by Austin innkeeper Richard Bullock, of the French minister's servant for killing Bullock's pigs. On September 10, 1842, Mexican General Adrian Woll captured San Antonio. He withdrew, taking everyone he had found in the district court: Judge Hutchinson was imprisoned at Perote until March, 1843. He then moved back to Mississippi.

The county was organized in 1901. Some historians believe Hutchinson County was the location of Quivira, the rich city described to Francisco Vasquez de Coronado in 1541 by an Indian who hoped to get the Spaniards out of New Mexico. Both battles of Adobe Walls were fought in Hutchinson County.

There was a courthouse at Plemmons prior to construction, in 1927, of the present $341,000 structure at Stinnett.

IRION COUNTY, MERTZON. Robert Anderson Irion, a Tennessean and Transylvania University graduate, was practicing medicine at Nacogdoches when the revolution began. He was a senator of the Republic and Houston's secretary of state.

Sherwood was the county seat when Irion County was organized in 1889. The coming of the railroad in 1910 resulted in the building of Mertzon, which became the county seat in the late 1930's. The second Irion County courthouse cost $60,000 in 1937.

JACK COUNTY, JACKSBORO. A University of Georgia graduate, William Jack moved to Texas in 1830. He was among those who opposed Mexican Colonel John Davis Bradburn, who had imprisoned his brother, Patrick Jack, and William Barret Travis. William Jack fought at San Jacinto, was David Burnet's secretary of state and a congressman of the Republic. Patrick Jack was a member of the Texas Congress and a district attorney.

The first settlement, in 1854, was Salt Hill. Jack County was organized three years later from Cooke County territory. The county seat was Lost Creek, which became Mesquiteville, Jacksborough, and Jacksboro. The present courthouse is Jack County's fourth. It cost $200,000 in 1940.

JACKSON COUNTY, EDNA. Originally a Mexican municipality, Jackson County was named for Andrew Jackson. It was created as a county in 1836. Texana—which had been Santa Anna until the Texans fell out of love with the Mexican dictator—was the county seat. Edna grew out of a commissary for Italian laborers on the New York, Texas and Mexican Railway line. It was first called Macaroni Station, then Edna for the daughter of railroad builder Joseph Telferner. The railroad missed Texana, and the county seat was moved to Edna in 1883. A courthouse was built there in 1884. The present courthouse is probably Jackson County's fourth. It was built in 1953 for $376,000.

JASPER COUNTY, JASPER. Jasper County honors William Jasper, who served under American Revolutionary general Francis Marion. It was part of Lorenzo de Zavala's empresario grant and before independence was in Bevil municipality. Jasper County was organized in December, 1836. John Bevil's homesite became the county seat and was named Jasper. Stephen Williams, the only soldier of the American Revolution known to have died in Texas, is buried at Jasper.

A log courthouse served from 1837 until it burned in 1848 and was replaced by a frame building. The present courthouse was built in 1885 at a cost of about $20,000.

JEFF DAVIS COUNTY, FORT DAVIS. When Jeff Davis County was formed out of Presidio County in 1887 a supporter said, "Thank God, we at last have a county named in honor of the president of the Confederacy." A prior attempt to honor Jefferson Davis had failed when, after the Civil War, Davis County had become Cass County again.

Fort Davis, which had grown up next to the military post ordered established by Secretary of War Jefferson Davis in 1854, was the capital of Presidio County, but since it lay within the new county, Jeff Davis County inherited the adobe courthouse that had been built for $2,400 in 1880. The new commissioners' minutes noted that "all records, books, and furniture except five iron cages and a scaffold at the jail" had been taken to the new Presidio County seat, Marfa. The existing $47,000 stone building replaced the first courthouse—called the Bat Cave—in 1910.

JEFFERSON COUNTY, BEAUMONT. The Mexican municipality of Jefferson was named for Thomas Jefferson. Jefferson County was one of the original counties of the Republic. The first settlement had been made in 1824 at Tevis Bluff. Noah Tevis, the first permanent settler, sold what became the Beaumont townsite. It was either named for the purchaser's kinsman, Jefferson Beaumont or for the rise a short distance from the site that was called beau mont, meaning "pretty hill."

Jefferson was the first county seat, succeeded by Beaumont in 1838. The present million dollar, multi-storied courthouse is Jefferson County's third. It was dedicated in 1932.

JIM HOGG COUNTY, HEBRONVILLE. James Stephen Hogg was the son of Brigadier General Joseph Hogg, who died early in the Civil War. Jim Hogg was a crusading attorney general who became Texas' first native born governor in 1891. The Railroad Commission was established in his administration. Later he was active in the oil business.

Mexican ranches were established in the county in the 18th century but Indians drove out the owners long before the Mexican War. Resettlement began after the Civil War. Jose and Ignacio Benavides arrived in 1868 to reclaim land the king of Spain had granted their grandfather in 1740. Part of the grant was sold to James R. Hebbron, a native of England, and became the Hebbronville site.

Jim Hogg County was created from parts of Brooks and Duval counties in 1913. Hebbronville is the county seat. The original courthouse is still in use. It cost $30,000 in 1913.

JIM WELLS COUNTY, ALICE. James B. Wells, of Georgia, captained steamboats on the Mississippi and Red rivers, fought in the Texas Revolution, and commanded a Texas Navy vessel. His son, James B. Wells, Jr., for whom the county is named, practiced law in Brownsville. For many years he helped former steamboatman Richard King put together the King Ranch. Alice, the county seat, was named for Alice Gertrudis King Kleberg, Captain King's daughter.

Jim Wells County was organized in 1912 and has had only the existing courthouse. Seventy thousand dollars worth of bonds were voted for the courthouse and jail. In 1912, when the cornerstone was laid, some 2,000 people came from all over South Texas for festivities which included a barbecue and goat roping.

JOHNSON COUNTY, CLEBURNE. South Carolinian Middleton Tate Johnson was an Alabama legislator who came to Texas in 1840. He was in the Texas Congress and fought in the Mexican War. For his services Johnson was granted land in frontier Tarrant County and was active in its organization. He was a delegate to the secession convention. Johnson County was organized in 1854. The county seat was to be named Wardville. Because Wardville was not sufficiently near the county's center, Buchanan succeeded it in 1856. But after Hood County was formed from Johnson County territory, Buchanan was no longer in the center of the county. In March, 1867, Camp Henderson became the seat of government. Its name was changed to honor Confederate General Patrick Cleburne. The present courthouse is the fourth in Cleburne. It was built in 1913 at a cost of $226,000.

JONES COUNTY, ANSON. President Anson Jones was born in Massachusetts January 20, 1798. Licensed in New York to practice medicine, he did not prosper. He practiced and taught school in Philadelphia, then was in Venezuela for two years. Back in Philadelphia in 1827 he qualified for a degree from Jefferson Medical College. He was a New Orleans commission merchant in 1832 and moved to Brazoria the next year. After serving as an army surgeon during the revolution, Jones was congressman, minister to the United States, and Houston's secretary of state. Jones was the last president of the Republic. In 1835 he and four others established the first Masonic Lodge in Texas and he was the first Grand Master of Texas. He died by his own hand January 9, 1858, in Houston.

Jones County was organized in 1881. Jones City, the county seat, changed its name to Anson the following year. Three courthouses preceded the present $300,000 structure, built in 1910.

KARNES COUNTY, KARNES CITY. Henry Wax Karnes, of Tennessee, was in the Battle of Concepción, the siege of Bexar, and was a scout at San Jacinto. In 1837, he was sent to Matamoras to exchange some Mexican prisoners. The Mexicans imprisoned him, but he escaped. Later he was an Indian fighter.

Spanish land grants in Karnes County date from 1758, but the Indians caused the county to be abandoned in the next century. The first permanent settlement in 1852, was at Helena, built on the site of Alamita, an old Mexican village.

Karnes County was created out of Bexar and Goliad counties in 1854. Helena, the county seat, began to decline after the railroad missed it in 1885. The county seat was moved in 1894 to a settlement on the right of way known as St. Joe and Cestahowa: it was renamed Karnes City. The old courthouse at Helena still stands. The Karnes City capitol was built in 1894 at a cost of $45,000.

KAUFMAN COUNTY, KAUFMAN. Pennsylvanian David Spangler Kaufman studied law in Mississippi and began practicing in Natchitoches, Louisiana in 1835. Two years later he moved to Nacogdoches. He took part in the Cherokee campaign and was wounded in the battle in which Chief Bowles was killed. He was speaker of the house of the Republic and became Texas' first United States congressman.

Kaufman County was formed out of Henderson County in 1848. The first county seat was Kingsborough, renamed Kaufman. A blacksmith shop accomodated county offices for awhile. In 1885 a courthouse was built which was replaced, in 1956, by the present $600,000 courthouse and jail.

KENDALL COUNTY, BOERNE. In 1837 George Wilkins Kendall founded the New Orleans *Picayune*. Later he joined the Santa Fe expedition to provide copy for his newspaper. He and the other participants were captured and imprisoned in Mexico. His *Narrative of the Santa Fe Expedition* is one of the great books of the Southwest. He lived in Texas while he wrote a book about his experiences as a correspondent in the Mexican War. After awhile in Europe in 1857 he bought a Kendall County ranch and there he died in 1867.

Kendall County was organized in 1862, the only one formed during the Civil War. Boerne was named for German poet and historian Ludwig Boerne, who was then a refugee in Texas. The present courthouse was built in 1870. Its cost was $3,285. Substantial additions have been made, and the courthouse was remodeled in 1954.

KENEDY COUNTY, SARITA. Mifflin Kenedy, a Pennsylvania Quaker, captained steamboats on the Ohio and Mississippi rivers. While in Florida he met Richard King. They began operating steamboats on the Rio Grande to supply American troops during the Mexican War. They added ranching to their other ventures. When they dissolved the ranching partnership it required thirteen months to divide all their property. Kenedy's La Parra Ranch was in Kenedy County.

The county was organized in 1921. The county seat was Sarita, named for Mifflin Kenedy's granddaughter, Sara. The county has had only one courthouse. It cost $48,000 in 1922 and has been twice remodeled.

KENT COUNTY, JAYTON. Kent County is named for Andrew Kent, a Gonzales resident when William Barret Travis sent for aid. Kent was one of the 32

Gonzales men who died in the fall of the Alamo on March 6, 1836.

Kent County was organized in 1892 with Clairemont the county seat. In 1954 Jayton won an election for removal of the county government. The present $500,000 courthouse, completed in 1957, is Jayton's first and Kent County's second.

KERR COUNTY, KERRVILLE. Kentucky-born James Kerr was a Missouri sheriff and legislator. A friend of Stephen Austin, Kerr arrived in Brazoria in 1825. He was the surveyor for the colonies of Green DeWitt and Benjamin Milam. As a Texas Congressman he authored legislation moving the capital from Houston to Austin. In his last years he practiced medicine.

The first settlers were shingle makers who established Brownsborough, which became Kerrville. Kerr County was organized in 1856. Kerrville was the first county seat. Comfort won an 1860 county seat election, but Kerrville became the county seat again in 1862 when Comfort became part of Kendall County. The present courthouse, of 1926 vintage, is Kerr County's fourth, and with the jail, cost $80,000.

KIMBLE COUNTY, JUNCTION. Kimble County honors George C. Kimbell—the difference in spelling reflects the uncertainty which has always existed over the correct spelling of Kimbell's name—who was living in Gonzales when William Barret Travis called for aid. Kimbell and thirty-one others crossed Mexican lines on March 1, 1836, to enter the Alamo. All were killed when the Alamo fell five days later.

Settlement began just before the Civil War, but the Indians kept the population down to a few ranchers and sheepmen. Kimble County was organized in 1876. Kimbleville was the county seat for a year and was succeeded by Junction City. The 1878 two-story frame courthouse burned nine years later. The present courthouse, the county's third, was built in 1929 for some $100,000.

KING COUNTY, GUTHRIE. Twenty-four year old William P. King lived in Gonzales when Alamo commander William Barret Travis sent for help. King and his brother, John C., were among the Gonzales men who arrived in time to perish with the other Alamo defenders March 6, 1936.

King County is ranching country—it was home to the Pitchfork, the 6666, and the Matador—and was slow to develop. Created in 1876 it had only forty residents in 1880. The population reached 173 in 1890, and the county was organized the following year when Guthrie bested Ashville to become the county seat. Two courthouses, one lost to a tornado and the other to fire, preceded the present building, which cost some $17,000 in 1914.

KINNEY COUNTY, BRACKETTVILLE. Pennsylvanian Henry Lawrence Kinney was one of Texas' great wheeler-dealers. He became known as Colonel Kinney in Illinois, reached Texas in 1838, and two years later was operating at Corpus Christi, which he helped found. He was a Texas congressman, a delegate to the 1845 convention, and an aide to Governor Henderson in the Mexican War. In 1852 he staged the first state fair, promoting it as far away as Europe. He advertised for settlers, calling Corpus Christi "the Naples of America." In 1854 he tried to establish a colony in Nicaragua. Because of his opposition to secession, he resigned from the Texas legislature in 1861. He was killed at Matamoras.

In 1834 J. C. Beales and James Grant tried to found a settlement, but it failed. Fort Clark was established in 1852, and enough settlers moved in so that Kinney County could organize in 1869. Oscar Brackett's trading post became a point on the San Antonio-El Paso stage and the village which developed became the county seat, Brackettville. Two courthouses preceded the present one, built in 1910 for $44,500.

KLEBERG COUNTY, KINGSVILLE. Robert Justus Kleberg was born in Germany and received the Juris Doctor degree from the University of Goettingen. He reached Texas in 1834 and was in the battle of San Jacinto. His son, Robert Justus Kleberg, was one of Richard King's attorneys, married King's daughter, Alice Gertrudis King, and managed the ranch after Richard King's death. The county seat, Kingsville, is located on the original tract of the King Ranch.

Kleberg County was organized in 1913. The $125,000 courthouse has served since 1914. It was remodeled and a wing was added in 1966.

KNOX COUNTY, BENJAMIN. Knox County was named for George Washington's first secretary of war, Henry Knox. It was created in 1858, then recreated in 1876. Knox County was mainly ranching country, but Robert Goree, a cattleman, began promoting the settlement of farmers in 1882. Knox County was organized in 1886. Benjamin was the county seat. In 1895 a colony of German immigrants established Rhineland. There have been only two courthouses: the present one cost $160,000 and was built in 1935.

LAMAR COUNTY, PARIS. Mirabeau Buonaparte Lamar was secretary to Georgia's Governor George Troup. He was a newspaperman and state senator, and after his wife's death he ran for Congress and was defeated. Lamar joined the Texas Army after Goliad, and commanded the cavalry at San Jacinto. He was Houston's vice president. As president he made Austin—well beyond the frontier—the capital. He was a lieutenant colonel in the Mexican War and died near Richmond in 1859.

Lamar County was created out of Red River County in 1841. A small plank courthouse at Lafayette served for two years, then a place called Mount Vernon was the county seat, a tavern serving as the courthouse. In 1844 Paris, which had been called Pinhook, was made the county seat. A log cabin courthouse was built about 1846, in the center of the square, followed by a two-story brick building. A larger brick courthouse was erected north of the square in 1873. It was replaced in 1895 by a granite building which burned in 1916. The present granite courthouse cost $175,000 in 1917.

LAMB COUNTY, LITTLEFIELD. George A. Lamb, of South Carolina, came to Walker County, in 1834. A second lieutenant, he was killed in the battle of San Jacinto, April 21, 1836.

Lamb County was created in 1876 but was organized late since much of it was occupied by the Yellow House and Spring Lake divisions of the XIT Ranch. As ranch lands were sold off to farmers, organization became possible in 1908. Olton, home of the Burro School, which acquired that name after a herd of burros froze to death there in a blizzard, was the county seat. The courthouse burned in 1922. After several unsuccessful attempts, Littlefield became the seat of government in 1946.

George Washington Littlefield was a Ranger, Confederate soldier, cattleman, and banker. He had extensive ranching interests in the panhandle and New Mexico. He founded Austin's American National Bank and was a substantial supporter of the state university.

The Olton courthouse was converted into a hospital. The present courthouse at Littlefield is Lamb County's third. It was built in 1953 and cost $240,000.

LAMPASAS COUNTY, LAMPASAS. Lampasas County—lampasas is Spanish for lilies—was named for the Lampasas River. Some of the early settlers came to the country believing that the water had medicinal qualities. Moses Hughes arrived in 1853, hoping his wife's health would be restored. The county was organized in 1856 when it was still on the frontier. Burleson became county seat and was renamed Lampasas. The present 1883 model courthouse is Lampasas County's second. It cost some $30,000 and was renovated in 1936.

LA SALLE COUNTY, COTULLA. Réne Robert Cavelier. Sieur de la Salle, was born in Rouen, France, November 22, 1643. He came to Canada when he was twenty-three, and in 1682 he explored the Mississippi River to the Gulf, claiming the region for France and naming it Louisiana for Louis XIV. The French king then gave La Salle permission to locate a colony at the mouth of the Mississippi, but he missed his destination and landed his colonists in Texas, probably on Matagorda Bay, in February, 1685. When Fort St. Louis, his settlement, was failing he went for help. One of his men killed him in March, 1687, in Grimes County or Cherokee County.

Joe Cotulla, who was born in Poland, started ranching in La Salle County before the Civil War. Although the county was created in 1858, Indian raids continued until 1878. The railroad came the next year and La Salle County was organized in 1880. La Salle, a settlement that had grown up at Fort Ewell, was the county seat for a short time and was succeeded by Cotulla. The largest roundup of mustangs in Texas took place near Cotulla. One thousand wild horses were captured for sale to the Argentine government. Three courthouses preceded the present one, which cost $63,000 in 1931.

LAVACA COUNTY, HALLETTSVILLE. The first Spaniards referred to the buffalo as cows, las vacas. Probably there were buffalo grazing along the river when the first Spanish explorer named it Lavaca. The county was named for the Lavaca River, which flows through Lavaca County.

Settlement began in the twenties. Lavaca County lay partly in the DeWitt colony and partly in the Austin colony. Lavaca was organized in 1846. After two bitter elections Hallettsville was chosen over Petersburg to be the county seat. Three courthouses preceded the 1897 structure which cost $77,925 and still serves the county.

LEE COUNTY, GIDDINGS. Lee County was named for Confederate General Robert Edward Lee, a West Pointer and Virginian who was stationed in Texas when the southern states began seceding in 1861. First offered command of the Union Army, he chose to stand by Virginia and became the greatest of the Southern commanders. Afterward he was president of Washington College, which became Washington and Lee University upon his death in 1870.

Lee County was created in 1874. Giddings, the county seat, was named for

J. D. Giddings, a member of the Somervell Expedition and the lawyer who established Brenham's first bank and built the Washington County Railroad.

The 1897 vintage courthouse that serves Lee County cost $32,270 and is the county's second. The first, built in 1878, burned nineteen years later.

LEON COUNTY, CENTERVILLE. Leon County may have been named for a yellow wolf that roamed that area and was called the lion or leon, or it may have been named for empresario Martin de León. It was part of the Mexican grant made to Austin and Williams.

Fort Boggy, a blockhouse, was the first settlement, built about 1840. Leon County was organized in 1846. Leona was the county seat until 1851, when the capital was moved to Centerville. The first courthouse was succeeded in 1858 by a brick building that burned in 1886: the present courthouse was built that year.

LIBERTY COUNTY, LIBERTY. Spaniards were in Liberty County searching for La Salle's colony in the late 1680's. In 1817 some of Napoleon's marshals tried to establish a colony near present Liberty. The municipality Villa de la Santisima Trinidad de la Libertad was established in 1831. Liberty, on the site of the old Spanish settlement Atascosito, was the capital.

After independence Liberty was one of the original counties of the Republic. A log courthouse, erected in 1837, burned in 1874. Sam Houston was one of the lawyers who practiced there. Three buildings preceded the present courthouse, which cost $208,000 in 1933. It was remodeled and an annex was built in 1957 at a cost of some $500,000.

LIMESTONE COUNTY, GROESBECK. Limestone County was organized in 1846, ten years after a Comanche war party carried away Cynthia Ann Parker and her brother, John, from Fort Parker. Springfield was the first county seat. The Houston and Texas Central Railroad reached Limestone County in 1869. Groesbeeck was founded along the right of way: Abram Groesbeeck was a railroad director. Springfield began to decline and in 1873 the county government was moved to Groesbeeck. (In 1900 the spelling was simplified to Groesbeck.) The current Limestone County courthouse was built in 1924 and cost in excess of $200,000.

LIPSCOMB COUNTY, LIPSCOMB. Abner Smith Lipscomb, a South Carolinian, studied law in John C. Calhoun's office. He was chief justice of the Alabama Supreme Court and came to Texas in 1839. Lipscomb was Lamar's secretary of state and a member of the 1845 constitutional convention. In 1846, Governor Henderson appointed him to the Texas Supreme Court.

Lipscomb County was ranching country after the buffalo were gone. With the coming of the railroad substantial settlement began. Organization occurred in 1887 with Lipscomb the county seat. The present $36,000 courthouse is the second for the county and was built in 1916.

LIVE OAK COUNTY, GEORGE WEST. Live Oak County was within the grants made to the Irish empresarios, John McMullen and James McGloin. Organized in 1856, the county is named for the live oak groves common to the area. Oakville was the county seat until the railroad came. The specifications for the first courthouse, in 1857, provided for 18-inch outside walls and 14-inch interior walls.

It cost $7,000 and was rebuilt in 1879. A public well was drilled for $30 in 1881. The Oakville square was fenced and had turnstiles: in time the board fence was replaced by smooth wire.

In 1918 George West offered to pay $75,000 of the cost if the county would build a new courthouse in his town. In the following election the voters decided to move to George West and the present $165,000 building was erected in 1919.

LLANO COUNTY, LLANO. Llano County's first settlers were Germans brought in by the Adelsverein. In 1845 John O. Meusebach made a treaty with the Comanches, giving the Indians presents in return for peace. Two years later Castell, a German community, became the first settlement.

Llano County was created from Bexar and Gillespie counties and was organized in 1856 with Llano—which means, in Spanish, plains—the county seat. The original frame courthouse burned in 1880. The present $34,500 building was erected in 1892.

LOVING COUNTY, MENTONE. Oliver Loving was one of the earliest and most important of the drovers, establishing three trails out of Texas, the Shawnee Trail, another that parallelled but preceded the Western Trail, and the Goodnight-Loving Trail to Colorado. Born in Kentucky, he came to Texas in 1846. He started trailing cattle in 1858 and was Charlie Goodnight's partner in 1867 when he died in New Mexico of wounds received in an Indian fight.

Loving, in 1931, was the last county organized. Mentone, the only town, is the county seat. It has the smallest population of any county in the nation, about 150 residents. There is no physician or hospital in the county, only one church and two organizations, the 4-H club and the Historical Survey Committee. Junior and senior high school students are sent to Wink, and three teachers educate the 21 younger children.

The first courthouse was built in 1931 and served until the present capitol was erected in 1936 at a cost of $25,000.

LUBBOCK COUNTY, LUBBOCK. Thomas S. Lubbock was the younger brother of Civil War Governor Francis Lubbock. Tom Lubbock, of South Carolina, joined the New Orleans Greys and took part in the siege of Bexar. He was a member of the Santa Fe Expedition in 1841, was captured, marched to Mexico City, and escaped. He also took part in the Somervell Expedition. In the Civil War he took command of Terry's Texas Rangers after Terry's death, but died the following month.

George Singer, probably the first settler, built a store in 1879 northwest of present Lubbock, the only business establishment and the only post office on the south plains. Singer moved into Lubbock in 1891 when the county was organized and Lubbock became the county seat.

The first courthouse was a $12,000 frame building. A 1915 yellow brick cost $100,000. The present courthouse was begun in 1950. The first part cost $1.2 million and the second, in 1968, $900,000.

LYNN COUNTY, TAHOKA. Lynn County was named for Alamo defender W. Lynn. The census showed nine residents in 1880 and seventeen in 1900. Near the center of the county is Tahoka Lake, fed by a spring. It was a natural camp site for Indians, buffalo hunters, soldiers, and wagon trains. Tahoka was an Indian word meaning deep or clear water.

The county was organized in 1903. Tahoka became the county seat in 1906. The Lynn County courthouse was built in 1916 and cost $73,547. It is the second for the county.

McCULLOCH COUNTY, BRADY. Ben McCulloch, a Tennessean and friend of David Crockett, participated in the battle of San Jacinto and was a member of the Texas Congress. He was a Ranger and served under General Zachary Taylor during the Mexican War. For two years he was sheriff of Sacramento County, California. President Franklin Pierce made him a United States Marshal, and President James Buchanan commissioned him to negotiate a peace with the Mormons in Utah. McCulloch, a Confederate brigadier general, was killed by sharpshooters at the Battle of Elk Horn.

McCulloch County was created from Bexar County while it was still buffalo country. It was organized in 1876 with Brady the county seat. One courthouse preceded the present building, which cost $37,000 in 1899.

McLENNAN COUNTY, WACO. Neil McLennan was born on the Isle of Sky in Scotland. He lived in North Carolina and Florida. With his brothers, John and Laughlin, he settled in present Falls County in 1835. Then Indians killed Laughlin McLennan, his wife and mother, and captured three of his children. In 1838, Indians killed John McLennan. Neil McLennan came into McLennan County as a member of George B. Erath's Ranger company and settled there in 1845.

Erath laid out Waco in 1849 on an old Waco Indian camp site. The sponsors called it Lamartine, but Erath insisted that it be named Waco Village. In 1850 McLennan County was organized with Waco Village the capital. Two courthouses preceded the present $100,000 building. On June 27, 1901, an estimated 10,000 visitors were in Waco to attend three events: the leveling of the courthouse cornerstone, the opening of the M K & T depot, and the commencement of a suspension bridge across the Brazos. Later a $700,000 courthouse annex was constructed.

McMULLEN COUNTY, TILDEN. John McMullen was born in Ireland in 1785. He lived in Baltimore, was a Matamoras merchant, and in 1829 became an empresario with James McGloin, his son-in-law. He was active in the Texas provisional government and was a San Antonio alderman after selling McGloin his San Patricio holdings.

McMullen County was organized in 1862, but outlaws were so troublesome and the population so small that the organization was abandoned. Vigilantes brought order and the county was reorganized in 1877. Dog Town became Tilden and was made the county seat. The original courthouse burned in 1929 and the existing $45,000 building was completed the following year.

MADISON COUNTY, MADISONVILLE. The county was named for President James Madison. An early Mexican settlement at Trinidad was destroyed by the Gutiérrez-Magee expedition of 1813. Settlement by Americans began in the 1820's.

The county was created from Grimes, Walker, and Leon counties in 1853. Madisonville is the county seat. Two courthouses preceded the $22,500 building erected in 1896, which burned May 14, 1967. A new courthouse was completed in 1970.

MARION COUNTY, JEFFERSON. Marion County was named for General Francis Marion of the American Revolution. It was created out of Cass County and organized in 1860. Jefferson, the county seat, was founded in 1836: it was first the Jefferson County capital, and from 1843 to 1852 was the seat of Cass County. For many years Jefferson was the most important city in north and east Texas. The Red River was obstructed, making Big Cypress Bayou navigable. Steamboats connected Jefferson and New Orleans by way of the Red and Mississippi rivers. Jefferson was second only to Galveston in size and importance in the 1860's and 1870's.

The present courthouse is Marion County's second. It cost $41,000 in 1912.

MARTIN COUNTY, STANTON. Wylie Martin, of Georgia, joined the army in 1805, was a scout for General William Henry Harrison and fought under General Andrew Jackson at Horseshoe Bend. After killing a man in a duel, he resigned his commission and came to Texas in 1823. He signed the Turtle Bayou resolutions, fought in the revolution, and was a senator of the Republic.

The first settlers were German Catholics who arrived in 1881. Martin County was organized in 1884: the county seat was Mariensfield, or field of Mary. Later Protestant settlers changed the name to Stanton. The original adobe courthouse was replaced by a two-story building, which gave way to the present $30,000 courthouse in 1908.

MASON COUNTY, MASON. Fort Mason was established in 1851 by United States dragoons. It was commanded at different times by Civil War generals Albert Sidney Johnston, George Thomas, Earl Van Dorn, and Robert E. Lee.

Mason County was created from Gillespie County and organized in 1858. Mason, which had grown up next to Fort Mason, was the county seat . The Mason County War was a feud that lasted through 1875 and 1876 and began with the lynching of five men for cattle rustling. The third Mason County courthouse was built in 1909 and cost $39,000.

MATAGORDA COUNTY, BAY CITY. Matagorda means dense cane and refers to the canebrakes Spaniards found near Matagorda Bay. La Salle was in Matagorda County in 1685. Some of Austin's colonists arrived there in 1822. The town of Matagorda, founded in 1829, had 1400 residents three years later.

Matagorda County was one of the original twenty-three counties of the Republic. Matagorda was succeeded as county seat by Bay City in 1894. The first Bay City courthouse was erected in 1895. The present $1.6 million building was occupied in 1965.

MAVERICK COUNTY, EAGLE PASS. Samuel Augustus Maverick, a Yale graduate, practiced law in South Carolina and Alabama. He was at the siege of Bexar and signed the Declaration of Independence. A former San Antonio mayor, he was among those seized by Mexican general Adrian Woll at the district court and taken to Mexico in August, 1842. Maverick, while in a Mexican prison, was elected to the Texas Congress. After secession he was in the group that pressed General D. E. Twiggs to surrender all United States Army property in Texas.

Most of the Spanish explorers came into Texas through Maverick County. The Camino Real, also called the old San Antonio Road and the King's Highway, was laid out in 1691 to connect San Juan Bautista with the recently established missions in East Texas. The Camino Real passed through Maverick County, and one of those who traveled it was Samuel Maverick after he was taken prisoner by General Woll.

Maverick County was organized in 1871, fifteen years after it was created out of Kinney County. A military post was established on the Rio Grande during the Mexican War and was named Camp Eagle Pass by soldiers who noted an eagle flying over each day to its nest on the Mexican side. The post was abandoned in 1849 by which time the town of Eagle Pass, El Paso del Aguila, had come into being. Eagle Pass became the seat of justice upon organization of the county. The county rented temporary quarters until the present $20,489 courthouse was ready in 1885.

MEDINA COUNTY, HONDO. Alonso de Léon named the Medina River for Pedro Medina, a Spanish scholar. The Medina River cuts across Medina County, which was created from Bexar County in 1848. The first courthouse was built at Castroville, established by Henri Castro, a Frenchman of Portuguese extraction, in 1844. Castro's colonists were mainly from France.

Hondo became the county seat in 1892, and the $40,000 courthouse erected that year is still in use. Additions were made costing $65,000 in 1943.

MENARD COUNTY, MENARD. Canadian Michel B. Menard traded and trapped in the northwest, the Illinois country, the Arkansas country, and in Louisiana. A signer of the Texas Declaration of Independence, he was commissioned to seek a five million dollar loan for the Republic in 1836. Later he bought a league and a labor of land on Galveston Island and organized the Galveston City Company.

The establishment, in 1853, of Fort McKavett provided enough protection to encourage settlement. Menard County was created in 1858, but Indian troubles prevented organization for several years. In 1871 the fort was garrisoned again and the county was organized. The first term of court was held under a live oak tree at Menard, the county seat. A two-story courthouse was built in 1872. Menard County is using its third courthouse, a $200,000 structure built in 1931.

MIDLAND COUNTY, MIDLAND. Midland County is located halfway between Fort Worth and El Paso on the Texas and Pacific Railroad. After the Indians withdrew and the buffalo hunters and antelope were gone, the sheepmen became the first permanent settlers, in the early eighties. Midland County was created from Tom Green County and organized in 1895. At least two courthouses preceded the existing 1929 model, which cost $319,000.

MILAM COUNTY, CAMERON. Kentuckian Benjamin Rush Milam, a veteran of the War of 1812, was trading with Comanches in 1818 when he met David G. Burnet, who was living with the Indians. Milam was in the Long expedition, and in 1821 he joined the Mexican Army. He assisted in some of the empresario efforts. Near the conclusion of the siege of Bexar as the army was about to withdraw, Milam shouted, "Who will go into Bexar with old Ben Milam?" Some 300 volunteers joined him. Milam was killed on the third day of the assault, December 7, 1835.

Milam County was created in 1836 from Milam municipality. The county seat was Old Nashville, but after several counties had been carved from Milam County a new capital was needed near the center of the remaining territory. Cameron was founded in 1846. A 30 × 20 foot courthouse of rough board construction was the first building in the new town. The second courthouse, slightly more elaborate than the first, burned in 1874. By 1889 the third courthouse was worn out. The present $85,000 structure was built in 1892. Originally it had a clock tower with a blindfolded statue of Justice. The tower was removed in 1930 and the clock faces were mounted on the walls.

MILLS COUNTY, GOLDTHWAITE. Irish-born John T. Mills came to Clarksville, in 1837. He practiced law, was a district judge during the Republic, and made an unsuccessful race for governor in 1849.

The first settler, in 1856, was Jesse Hanna. The railroad arrived in 1886, and Mills was created from Brown County and three others the next year. Goldthwaite was the county seat. The existing courthouse is Mills County's second. It was completed in 1913 and cost $77,000.

MITCHELL COUNTY, COLORADO CITY. Pennsylvanians Asa and Eli Mitchell moved to Texas in the 1820's. Asa, an Austin colonist and member of the consultation, fought at San Jacinto. Eli Mitchell was at Gonzales in October, 1835 when the revolution began. He served three terms there as tax collector.

Mitchell County was created in 1876 but had only 117 residents in 1880. The Texas and Pacific Railroad arrived and the county was organized in 1881. The county seat was Colorado City, the oldest town on the T & P between Weatherford and El Paso. An 1877 Ranger camp site, the railroad made it the most important town in West Texas. Its population was 5,000 in 1882.

The county had two courthouses before the present $115,000 building was completed in 1924.

MONTAGUE COUNTY, MONTAGUE. Daniel Montague, of Massachusetts, surveyed in Louisiana and was a Fannin County merchant. He was a member of the Snively expedition in 1843 and served in the Mexican War. After the Civil War he lived in Mexico ten years, but he died in Cooke County, Texas, in 1876.

At Spanish Fort, Indians flying a French flag turned back a force of Spaniards led by Diego Ortiz Parrilla in 1759. Permanent settlement began in 1854, and Montague was carved out of Cooke County in 1857. The county was organized in 1858. Farmers Creek, Head of Elm, and a site that was to be named Montague were potential capitals. The courthouse at Montague, built of logs, served until after the Civil War. A stone building was then rented until it burned in 1873. The third courthouse, also of stone, burned in 1884. The existing 1912 vintage courthouse cost $40,000.

MONTGOMERY COUNTY, CONROE. The county, named for American Revolutionary hero General Richard Montgomery, was organized in 1837 with Montgomery the capital. The first courthouse, a two-room log cabin, was built in 1838. A two-story wooden building took its place in 1842. Willis was the county seat from 1874 to 1880 when Montgomery was again chosen. The county seat was moved to Conroe in 1889. The present courthouse is Montgomery County's sixth. It cost $379,000 in 1936 and was remodeled in 1965 at a cost of $750,000.

MOORE COUNTY, DUMAS. Edwin W. Moore, a Virginian, was an officer in the United States Navy when he resigned to command the Texas Navy in 1839. His first winter was spent in New York City enlisting sailors. He patrolled the Gulf in the tiny fleet until President Houston suspended Moore for disobedience in 1843. A court-martial convicted him of only minor charges. For years after the navy was dissolved, Moore argued the propriety of his actions and tried to collect sums he contended Texas owed him.

Moore County settlement came late: the 1892 population was 15, including the nine members of the Rob Spurlock family. Moore County was organized in 1892 with Dumas the county seat. Dumas had 23 residents in 1903. One courthouse preceded the $155,000 building erected in 1930 and presently in use.

MORRIS COUNTY, DAINGERFIELD. North Carolinian William Wright Morris studied law in Alabama and settled near Henderson, Texas, in 1847. As judge and legislator he promoted East Texas railroads.

There was settlement during the Republic sufficient for Congress to create Paschal County and make Daingerfield its capital. The supreme court declared judicial counties such as Paschal unconstitutional in 1842. Morris County was created from Titus County in 1875. Daingerfield bested Selma to become the county seat. The present courthouse was built in 1881 and cost $15,000.

MOTLEY COUNTY, MATADOR. Junius William Mottley, a Virginian, studied medicine at Transylvania University. He was appointed surgeon for Goliad in January of 1836. A signer of the Declaration of Independence, he was an aide to General T. J. Rusk when he was killed at San Jacinto.

Motley County—the legislative act misspelled Mottley's name—was created in 1876. Since it was mainly Matador Ranch grazing land, there was still no town in 1891. But a county seat town was necessary for organization, and the General Land Office apparently required that there be twenty businesses before a place could be considered a town. Matador Ranch hands set up twenty temporary stores using supplies from the ranch headquarters and called the community Matador. A patent was issued for the town of Matador, which became the county seat.

The present courthouse, built in 1948 for $225,000, is Motley County's second.

NACOGDOCHES COUNTY, NACOGDOCHES. The Nacogdoches Indians were of the Hasinai confederacy of the Caddo. The mission Nuestra Señora de Guadalupe de los Nacogdoches was established in 1716 at an Indian village where present Nacogdoches stands. In April, 1779 Nacogdoches was resettled by Gil Antonio Ibarbo and his followers.

Before the revolution, Texas was divided into three departments, everything east of the Trinity constituting the department of Nacogdoches. After the revolution Nacogdoches was one of the original counties: some twenty other counties were carved from it. In 1958 the present $600,000 courthouse was erected. At least two courthouses preceded it.

NAVARRO COUNTY, CORSICANA. José Antonio Navarro was active in the revolutionary activities of Magee and Gutiérrez. He and Austin met in 1821 and became close friends. In 1824 Navarro represented Texas in the legislature of Coahulia y Texas. He was a signer of the Declaration of Independence and a congressman of the Republic. A member of the Santa Fe expedition, he was imprisoned in Mexico City for more than three years. He was a delegate to the 1845 convention and a state senator.

Navarro County was organized in 1846. Corsicana, the county seat, honored Navarro's ancestry. His father was born on Corsica. A settler's home served the county until a log courthouse was constructed in 1848. The third courthouse, a two-story frame used from 1851 to 1855, was destroyed by fire. The fourth, in 1858, was of brick, and the fifth capitol cost $56,000 in 1880. The present $150,000 courthouse is of 1905 vintage.

NEWTON COUNTY, NEWTON. Newton County honors an American revolutionary soldier, Corporal John Newton, a friend of Sergeant William Jasper, for whom Jasper County was named. Jasper served in the regiment of General Francis Marion: Marion County commemorates his services.

Newton County, which had been part of Jasper County, was organized in July, 1846. Except for the period 1848 to 1853, when Burkeville was the capital, Newton has been the county seat. The third courthouse, built in 1902 at a cost of $25,000, is still in use.

NOLAN COUNTY, SWEETWATER. Philip Nolan, a native of Belfast, Ireland, was a protege of General James Wilkinson. When he was about twenty he came into Texas, mustanging and trading horses. He made several trips and because of his knowledge of Texas—he had executed what was probably the best map of the region—Spaniards feared that he might help someone seize Texas. Nolan's association with Wilkinson was reason enough for suspicion: while Wilkinson commanded the United States Army he was also a Spanish secret agent. In 1800 Nolan's arrest was ordered if he returned to Texas. He was killed near modern Waco by Spanish troops sent to arrest him.

Soon after Nolan County was created in 1876 Tom Knight opened a store in a dugout near Sweetwater Creek. His customers were buffalo hunters and then cowhands. The place was called Blue Goose because a raw cowhand from the east shot a blue crane there. His friends said it was a blue goose, so he cooked and ate it. Blue Goose became the Sweet Water post office, and upon the organization of the county in 1881, Sweetwater moved to the site selected for the county seat two miles away on the railroad. A shack served as the first courthouse. The second was a $20,000 rock building completed in 1882: the courthouse fell apart because of faulty mortar and cost $12,935 to rebuild from the old material in 1891. The present edifice was completed in 1917 at a cost of about $105,000.

NUECES COUNTY, CORPUS CHRISTI. Nueces County is named after the Nueces River, which Alonso de León named in 1689. Nueces means nuts. The Nueces is probably the stream Cabeza de Vaca called the River of Nuts a century and a half earlier.

Nueces County was visited by Alonso Alvarez de Piñeda in 1519. Henry Kinney began its permanent settlement in 1842. He promoted Corpus Christi as the

"Naples of America" and held the first state fair there. Corpus Christi was the seat of government when Nueces County was organized in 1846. The present $465,000 courthouse was built in 1914 and is the county's third. Additions were made in 1931 and 1961.

OCHILTREE COUNTY, PERRYTON. William Beck Ochiltree, of North Carolina, practiced law in Alabama. He came to Nacogdoches in 1839, and was a judge, secretary of the treasury, and adjutant general during the Republic. He was a secession delegate and resigned from the Confederate provisional congress to raise a cavalry regiment.

Ochiltree County was organized in 1889 with Ochiltree the capital. George Perry, an early settler, was both county clerk and judge. When the railroad was extended, a townsite on the right of way was named Perryton and made the county seat.

One courthouse existed prior to the present $93,000 building, completed in 1928.

OLDHAM COUNTY, VEGA. Williamson Simpson Oldham practiced law in Tennessee, was an Arkansas Supreme Court justice and speaker of the Arkansas House. He came to Texas in 1849, was co-publisher of a newspaper, and published a digest of the Texas statutes. Later he was a Confederate senator.

Tascosa became the capital upon the organization of Oldham County in 1880. After the decline of Tascosa, Vega became the county seat. The present $35,000 courthouse was built in 1915. The old courthouse at Tascosa was taken over in 1939 by Cal Farley's Boys Ranch and is operated as Julian Bivins Museum.

ORANGE COUNTY, ORANGE. The county was named for the orange groves near the mouth of the Sabine. Orange County was carved out of Jefferson County in 1852. Madison was the county seat, but because there was Madisonville and Madison County, it was renamed Orange. At first there was no courthouse, and court was held in the Masonic temple or out of doors. A one-story wooden building, the first courthouse was succeeded by a two-story edifice that burned in 1897. The present structure was built in 1937 and cost $200,000.

PALO PINTO COUNTY, PALO PINTO. One of the principal streams of the county is Palo Pinto—Painted Wood—Creek. Palo Pinto County was organized in 1857, soon after the first permanent settlers arrived. Oliver Loving and Charles Goodnight were among the early residents. In 1858 the legislature granted 320 acres of land for Golconda, the county seat: it became Palo Pinto the next year. The present courthouse, occupied in 1940, cost $220,000.

PANOLA COUNTY, CARTHAGE. Panola is an Anglicized version of the Indian word for cotton, ponolo. Panola County was created from Shelby and Harrison counties in 1846. Four courthouses preceded the present one, the first in 1848 was a log cabin and the second, in 1850, a frame building. In 1856 a brick courthouse was built, and in 1885 a many-turreted edifice of hand-made brick was erected. The present $600,000 Carthage courthouse is of 1953 vintage.

PARKER COUNTY, WEATHERFORD. Isaac Parker came from Georgia by way of Tennessee and Illinois and served in the army and the Texas Congress. As a state senator he introduced the bill which created Parker County. His brother, Silas, was killed in the Comanche raid on Fort Parker in 1836 when Silas' children, Cynthia Ann and John, were captured.

Parker County was created from Bosque and Navarro and organized in 1855. Weatherford, the county seat, honored Jefferson Weatherford, the state senator from Dallas. The first courthouse was of rough pine hauled from Red River County. The second, a two-story brick, burned in 1874. Ten years later the third building burned. The 1894 Parker County courthouse cost $55,555.55. A renovation in the middle fifties cost $158,000.

PARMER COUNTY, FARWELL. Martin Parmer, of Virginia, lived in Tennessee and was a Missouri state senator who called himself the "Ringtailed Panther from the Forks of the Creek." He participated in the Fredonian Rebellion and later signed the Declaration of Independence.

Most of Parmer County was within the XIT Ranch. The 70 residents shown by the 1890 census were XIT employees. The population was 34 in 1900, but it began to grow when the XIT was broken up for sale to farmers and small ranchers.

Parmer County was organized in 1907, and Farwell became the county seat. John V. Farwell was an officer of the Capitol Syndicate, the owner and operator of the XIT. Two courthouses preceded the present one, built in 1916 for $43,243.65.

PECOS COUNTY, FORT STOCKTON. The Pecos River rises in New Mexico and some 250 of its 800 miles is in that state. Part of the Pecos parallels the Rio Grande.

Pecos County was organized in 1875. Fort Stockton had been established in 1859, and the settlement which grew up near the military post became Fort Stockton, the Pecos County seat. The fort was garrisoned sporadically until 1886. One courthouse preceded the present structure, which was finished in 1911.

POLK COUNTY, LIVINGSTON. Polk County is heavily timbered. Its first permanent settlers were the Alabama-Coushatta Indians. Among the earliest white residents was Sam Houston.

The county was named for President James K. Polk. Carved from Liberty County, it was organized in 1846. Livingston won the county seat election from Swartwout: it was much closer to the center of the county than Swartwout. Two courthouses preceded the present building, erected in 1923.

POTTER COUNTY, AMARILLO. Robert Potter was a United States Navy midshipman, a lawyer, and a North Carolina congressman. He was sentenced to two years in jail for maiming his wife's cousin and another man. Afterward he was a North Carolina legislator until he was expelled in 1835 for "playing a game of cards unfairly, contrary to the rules." He served in T. J. Rusk's army and then in the Texas Navy. He signed the Declaration of Independence, was secretary of the navy, and was killed in the Regulator-Moderator troubles.

Potter County was still buffalo country when Casimir Romero brought in a herd of sheep in 1876. Potter County was organized in 1887, the year the railroad arrived, with Amarillo the county seat. The 1887 frame courthouse cost $924.60. A stone building costing $33,000 in 1888 was dedicated with a grand ball, a fine occasion for the eight women who attended, since more than a hundred men were there, some from 75 miles away. Amarillo moved a mile to a new site, and by an election in 1893 it was decided that the courthouse should be relocated there. County officers obtained temporary quarters, and the courthouse was torn down, moved, and rebuilt in 1895. A new courthouse was erected in 1905. The present temple of justice was completed in 1931 and cost $391,000.

PRESIDIO COUNTY, MARFA. Ranching was carried on in Presidio County by Indians and Mexicans before the arrival in 1854 of Milton Favor, the first Anglo-American rancher in the Big Bend.

Presidio County was first created from Santa Fe County in 1850 with Fort Leaton the county seat. No organization occurred, and in 1871 Pecos County was created from Presidio County territory. It was finally organized in 1875 with Fort Davis the county seat. In 1885 the capital was moved to Marfa: the name had been encountered in a Russian novel by the wife of the president of the Texas and New Orleans Railroad. The present courthouse cost some $100,000 in 1886.

RAINS COUNTY, EMORY. Emory Rains came to present Lamar County from Tennessee in 1826. He was a senator of the Republic and a state legislator. He helped survey Rains County, created from Hopkins, Hunt, and Wood counties in 1870, with Emory the county seat. Settlement had begun in the late 1840's. Rains County quickly outgrew its log courthouse and a two-room structure was erected. It burned in 1879 and temporary quarters were used until a two-story brick was erected in 1884. It burned in 1890. The present courthouse was built in 1908 for about $35,000.

RANDALL COUNTY, CANYON. Tennessee-born Horace Randal had lived in Texas since he was six years old. A West Pointer, he resigned from the army at secession. He was a Confederate brigadier general, killed April 30, 1864, in the battle of Jenkins' Ferry.

Randall County—the legislature misspelled the name in the act creating the county—was organized in 1889. The original settlers were ranchers who opposed county organization because it would encourage settlement. The 1880 census had listed only three residents of Randall County, Walter Dyer, 25, the brother-in-law of Charles Goodnight, described as a "stock grower;" William Lampton, 33; and Samuel Coleman, 21, both listed as "herding cattle."

Canyon City, at the headquarters of the T Anchor Ranch, was the county seat. Six of the first county officers were T Anchor employees. An $8,200 two-story frame courthouse, built in 1889, served as Sunday school, dance hall, school, wedding chapel and funeral parlor. The present courthouse is the fourth: it was built in 1968 at a cost of $400,000.

REAGAN COUNTY, BIG LAKE. Tennessean John H. Reagan came to Texas at twenty-one, served in the Cherokee war in the Lamar administration, was a surveyor, and a Nacogdoches County justice of the peace. He was Henderson County judge in 1846, and five years later was the district judge at Palestine. Before secession he was a congressman. He was the Confederate postmaster general and, for a time, secretary of the treasury. The United States imprisoned him for awhile after the war, but in 1875 he was elected to congress. In 1891, Jim Hogg persuaded Reagan to give up his seat in the United States Senate and become chairman of the new Railroad Commission. The entire Texas legislature attended John Reagan's funeral.

The Big Lake was the only fresh water for many miles. P. H. Coates built a house beside the lake in 1894: he had camped there for awhile in the eighties and thus had a claim to seniority as an old settler.

Reagan County was created in 1903. Stiles, with 75 residents, was the county seat in 1904. A native stone courthouse was erected there. The county seat was moved to Big Lake in 1925, and the courthouse completed in 1927 at a cost of $50,000 is still used.

REAL COUNTY, LEAKEY. Julius Real was the son of Casper Real, a native of Dusseldorf, Germany, and Emelie Schreiner, born in Alsace-Lorraine, and the sister of Charles Schreiner. The six Real brothers were leading hill country citizens. Julius Real was Kerr County judge and state senator: Real County was named for him.

John Leakey erected his house near present Leakey in Frio Canyon in 1857. Indian raids retarded settlement until 1881. Leakey was the seat of Edwards County from 1883 until 1913 when Real County was organized and Leakey became its capital. The present courthouse, built in 1917, is Real County's second and cost $12,000.

RED RIVER COUNTY, CLARKSVILLE. Americans began settling in Red River County in 1814. The boundary between Texas and Arkansas was uncertain, and this settlement was largely an extension of the movement into Arkansas. Many of the early residents of Red River County believed their farms were in Miller County, Arkansas. James Clark laid out Clarksville in 1833. When Red River County was organized in 1837 LaGrange—which later became Madras—was the county seat, a fact the county judge ignored as he held court in Clarksville. The contest between the two communities was not resolved until 1850 when Clarksville became the county seat permanently. Red River County's fifth courthouse was built for about $50,000 in 1884-85.

REEVES COUNTY, PECOS. George R. Reeves, of Tennessee, moved to Grayson County, Texas where he was tax collector, sheriff, and legislator. He was a Confederate colonel and later was speaker of the Texas House.

Settlement in Reeves County was slight before the railroad came in 1881. Reeves was formed from Pecos County two years later. Toyah and Pecos City were prospective county seats in an 1884 election: 253 votes were cast, but some questioned how many of the voters were children and non-residents. Finally the ballots were taken to Fort Stockton to be counted and Pecos City was declared the winner. The present courthouse, the county's second, was built in 1937 at a cost of $120,000.

REFUGIO COUNTY, REFUGIO. The last Texas mission, Nuestra Señora del Refugio, was established in present Calhoun County in 1793 and moved the next year to the site of modern Refugio.

In 1834 the Irish empresarios Power and Hewetson founded Refugio and brought in colonists from Ireland and Mexico. The municipality of Refugio became one of the original counties of the Republic. Refugio County was organized in 1837 with Refugio the county seat. Several counties were created from its territory, and in 1869 St. Marys became the county seat. The legislature designated Rockport as the county capital in 1871, but because of the controversy the legislature then created Aransas County, made Rockport its seat of government, and moved Refugio County government back to Refugio. The present courthouse cost $75,000, is the county's third, and was built in 1919. A $350,000 addition and remodeling was completed in 1950.

ROBERTS COUNTY, MIAMI. Roberts County honors John S. Roberts and Oran M. Roberts. John S. Roberts, a Virginian, supported the Fredonian Rebellion, served in the Texas Army, and signed the Declaration of Independence. South Carolinian O.M. Roberts was a Texas Supreme Court justice, chairman of the secession convention and colonel of a Confederate infantry regiment, and chief justice of the Texas Supreme Court. After the Civil War, he was elected to the United States Senate, but the radical Republicans would not seat him. Later he was governor and one of the first members of the University of Texas faculty.

The railroad reached Roberts County in 1887, and the county was organized in 1889, thirteen years after its creation. Supporters of Parnell and Miami contested for the county seat. Miami citizens chose officials. They bought furniture and a safe which were captured and taken to Parnell where a courthouse was built around the safe. Parnell was the capital until an 1898 election so designated Miami. The present courthouse was finished in 1913 and cost $43,000.

ROBERTSON COUNTY, FRANKLIN. Sterling Clack Robertson, a Tennessean and veteran of the War of 1812, was a member of the Nashville Company, which was formed for Texas colonization. In 1825 Mexico granted permission to the company to settle 800 families in an area which included present Robertson County. Robertson signed the Declaration of Independence and was a congressman of the Republic.

Old Franklin was the seat of government when Robertson County was organized in 1838, but after the county boundaries were changed Wheelock was more centrally located, and in 1850 a courthouse was built there. Owensville succeeded Wheelock in 1855. After five years Calvert became the capital. Finally, when the railroad arrived in 1879 county government was moved to Morgan—located on the railroad—which was renamed Franklin. The sixth Franklin County courthouse was built in 1883 at a cost of $30,000.

ROCKWALL COUNTY, ROCKWALL. Rockwall is the smallest Texas county, having an area of only 147 square miles. In 1852 the rock structure for which the county was named was examined by excavation. At one time it projected above the ground a foot or more in places. Settlement began in 1846. Because of the inconvenience of doing business at the seat of Kaufman County, residents asked that they have their own county government. Rockwall County was broken off Kaufman County and organized in 1873 with Rockwall the county seat. A store building became the first courthouse, but it burned in 1875. The second was a $3,940 building erected in 1878 on the present square. It burned in 1892. A two-story stone courthouse was built in 1892 for $25,000 and served until the present $100,000 structure was occupied in 1940.

RUNNELS COUNTY, BALLINGER. Hiram G. Runnels, a Georgian, served in the army and was a Mississippi legislator and governor. He moved to Texas in 1842 and represented Brazoria County in the 1845 convention.

Runnels County was created from Bexar and Travis counties in 1858 and organized in 1880. The first courthouse was located at Old Runnels. The Santa Fe railroad crossed the county in the eighties, and Ballinger, on the right of way, became the county seat. Most Old Runnels residents moved to Ballinger. A $29,000 courthouse was completed in 1889. It was remodeled in 1941 and still serves the county.

RUSK COUNTY, HENDERSON. In 1832 Thomas Jefferson Rusk, a South Carolinian, was defrauded by partners who fled to Texas. He followed them. Rusk was inspector general of the Texas Army, signed the Declaration of Independence, was secretary of war, and commanding general of the army. He was chief justice of the Texas Supreme Court, and he and Sam Houston were Texas' first United States senators.

Rusk was created from Nacogdoches County and organized in 1843. Henderson was the county seat. The first courthouse and most of the business section burned in 1860, and because of tensions caused by the secession question the fire resulted in violence. Rusk County's present courthouse is its fourth. It was built in 1928 and cost $243,650.

SABINE COUNTY, HEMPHILL. Sabine is the corruption of a Spanish word meaning cypress. When Domingo Ramón named the Sabine River in the early 18th century he was referring to the heavy growth of cypress trees on that stream.

Settlement began in Sabine County in 1819 and Sabine Municipality became one of the original counties of the Republic, organized in 1837. Milam was the county seat until 1858 when Hemphill was designated as the capital. The fourth courthouse is still in use. It was built in 1906 and cost $30,000. After a 1908 fire repairs were made. A remodeling was completed in 1938.

SAN AUGUSTINE COUNTY, SAN AUGUSTINE. The Moscoso expedition passed through San Augustine County in 1542. In 1716 the mission Nuestra Señora de los Dolores de los Ais was founded to minister to the Ais Indians. It was abandoned and then re-established in 1721 on the site of modern San Augustine. Antonio Leal was the first settler, in 1794. The municipality of San Augustine was established in 1834. It included all or part of six modern counties and had a population of 260 in 1835.

San Augustine County was one of the original counties of the Republic. San Augustine is the county seat. The present courthouse was built in 1927 at a cost of $100,000.

SAN JACINTO COUNTY, COLDSPRING. One explanation of the naming of the San Jacinto River was that when the Spaniards found it, the stream was so full of hyacinths that it was difficult to cross. Therefore it was named San Jacinto for St. Hyacinth. Another version was that the river was discovered on St. Hyacinth's Day, August 17.

San Jacinto County was organized in 1870. The county seat was first called Coonskin, then Fireman's Hill, Cold Spring, and finally Coldspring. When the original courthouse burned in 1915 Coldspring was relocated a short distance away. The second courthouse cost $57,632 in 1917.

SAN PATRICIO COUNTY, SINTON. The Irishmen John McMullen and James McGloin named their colony San Patricio for Ireland's patron, Saint Patrick. The first settlers, mostly Irish, arrived in 1830. There were about 500 residents in the colony when General Jose Urrea's forces surprised and defeated a small body of Texan troops in January, 1836. Because of the fighting, San Patricio settlers fled to Victoria. Most returned after San Jacinto.

San Patricio was one of the original counties. A courthouse was built at San Patricio Hibernia soon after the county organized in 1837. The courthouse burned during the Civil War and most of the records were lost. Sinton became the county seat in 1893. The present $125,000 courthouse was built in 1928. A $370,000 remodeling was done in the middle fifties.

SAN SABA COUNTY, SAN SABA. San Saba was created from Bexar County in 1856. Permanent settlement had begun about 1839. Rowe's Land was designated the first county seat, but six weeks later a special election moved the county government to the San Saba site. The 1857 courthouse, which had cost $850, was replaced with a stone building in 1871. Forty years thereafter the present $100,000 building was occupied.

SCHLEICHER COUNTY, ELDORADO. Gustav Schleicher, who had studied engineering and architecture at Germany's University of Giessen, was a founder of Bettina, a socialistic experiment that failed. He represented San Antonio in the legislature, was a Confederate captain, and died in Washington while serving in congress.

Even after the withdrawal of the Indians, Schleicher County's future was not promising because of the scarcity of surface water. Land sold in large tracts to unwary investors for a dime an acre. But the windmill changed all that. Schleicher County was created from Crockett County in 1887. The 1890 census showed 150 residents and as the twentieth century dawned there were 515. It was organized in 1901 with the county seat at Eldorado. One courthouse preceded the present one which was built in 1924 for $60,000.

SCURRY COUNTY, SNYDER. William R. Scurry, of Tennessee, was an aide to General T. J. Rusk and a congressman of the Republic. A Mexican War veteran and Confederate brigadier general, he died in the Battle of Jenkins' Ferry.

Scurry County was created in 1876 from Bexar County. In 1877 W. H. Snyder established a trading post that became a settlement bearing his name. The 1880 census showed 102 Scurry County residents. Upon organization, in 1884, Snyder became the county seat. A $25,000, two-story brick courthouse was dedicated northeast of the present square in 1886. That September the commissioners authorized construction of a hitching rail and a wooden sidewalk. In 1903 sponsors of a new courthouse said it would improve the county's chances of getting railroad service, but the railroad arrived before the new courthouse—the one still in use—was erected: it was begun in 1909 and completed in 1911 at a cost of $75,000.

SHACKELFORD COUNTY, ALBANY. John Shackelford, a Virginian and War of 1812 veteran, practiced medicine in South Carolina. As an Alabama state senator, he raised a company for the Texas Army, clothing them in red jeans. Many of these Red Rovers, as they styled themselves, were killed in the Goliad Massacre, but Shackelford was spared because physicians were needed to care for wounded Mexican troops. He died in Alabama in 1857.

Shackelford County settlement began in 1858. The William Ledbetter salt works, established in the early sixties, served a large market. Fort Griffin was established in 1867 to assist the Indian campaign of Colonel Ranald Mackenzie. Shackelford County was organized in 1874 with the county seat at the town of Fort Griffin, which had grown up next to the military post. The following year Albany became the capital. One courthouse preceded the present structure, built in 1883 at a cost of $49,000. During the terrible drought of 1886, an appeal for help was made to President Grover Cleveland and the American Red Cross, whose president, Clara Barton, visited Albany and then began a funds campaign in Dallas for the relief of the distressed area.

SHELBY COUNTY, CENTER. Shelby County, named for Isaac Shelby, a Tennessean who figured prominently in the American Revolution, was in the municipality of Tenaha. Settlement began early. John Latham was the first permanent resident, in 1818. Just to the east lay the Neutral Ground, resulting in a rather tough element in Shelby County, one of the original counties. Shelbyville was the first seat of Shelby County, succeeded by Center in 1866. The first Center courthouse burned in 1882. The present one, designed by an Irish architect, Jacob Joseph Emmett Gibson, cost approximately $26,000 in 1885.

SHERMAN COUNTY, STRATFORD. Massachusetts-born Sidney Sherman equipped fifty-two Kentucky volunteers and brought them to Texas, where he was one of Houston's commanders at San Jacinto.

Sherman County was created in 1876 and organized in 1889. Coldwater was the first county seat. The 1880 census reflected no population. Apparently the petition for organization contained some fraudulent entries. By law 150 residents were needed but in the year after Sherman County organized the census showed only 34 citizens. Stratford—named by an Englishman for Stratford-on-the-Avon, perhaps because both towns were located on creeks—became the capital in 1901. Coldwater citizens did not take kindly to the change—they had built a brick courthouse in 1891—and the tent in Stratford housing the county records was guarded by armed men pending completion of the courthouse. The first grand jury at Stratford indicted William Bonney, Billy the Kid. The present courthouse was built in 1922 at a cost of $62,500.

SMITH COUNTY, TYLER. A South Carolinian and War of 1812 veteran, James Smith moved to Nacogdoches in 1835 and became a Texas Army colonel. In 1844 President Houston sent him to Shelby County to stop the Regulator-Moderator War. He was a legislator when Smith County was created.

Smith County was occupied by Caddo Indians when the Cherokees moved in about 1818. Smith County was formed from Nacogdoches in 1846, with Tyler the capital. Three log courthouses preceded the first masonry building. A third floor was added to the masonry courthouse, then four smaller buildings were constructed, so that finally there were five structures on the square. In 1908 all county functions were housed in one building again. The present $1.5 million courthouse was occupied in 1955.

SOMERVELL COUNTY, GLEN ROSE. Alexander Somervell, of Maryland, fought at San Jacinto and became David G. Burnet's secretary of war. In 1842 Sam Houston put him in charge of what became the Somervell Expedition, a retaliatory move provoked by the invasions of Mexican generals Rafael Vasquez and Adrian Woll. Since Texas was in no position to fight a war, Houston may have intended the expedition as a safety valve, for Somervell disbanded his force at Laredo. William S. Fisher led 313 men in an attempt to capture the town of Mier. They were captured and marched toward Mexico City.

Somervell County was organized in 1875 with Glen Rose the capital. A log cabin was used for county business until 1882: the courthouse built that year burned in 1893 and was succeeded by the present one, which cost $13,500.

STARR COUNTY, RIO GRANDE CITY. James Harper Starr, of Connecticut, was a Georgia physician, a Texas General Land Office official, and Lamar's secretary of the treasury. Although he opposed secession he was later a Confederate agent.

Starr County settlement began in 1753, but the community on the site of Rio Grande City failed. Then Henry Clay Davis started a town in 1847 that he called Rancho Davis. Fort Ringgold, begun the next year, brought additional population, and Starr County was organized in 1848. The first courthouse was not situated on the square. Built in the 1850's, it is still used for some county functions. A two-story building erected on the square in the eighties was torn down when the present courthouse was built in 1939 for some $225,000.

STEPHENS COUNTY, BRECKENRIDGE. The county was created in 1858 and named Buchanan County for President James Buchanan. Breckenridge—honoring United States Senator John C. Breckenridge of Kentucky, who would run for president against Lincoln two years later—was to be the county seat. After secession the name of the county was changed to honor Confederate Vice President Alexander H. Stephens.

Stephens County was organized in 1876. At Breckenridge a building of pine boards served until a more substantial courthouse was built in 1883. The present county capitol was dedicated in 1926. The land, building, and furniture cost $454,222.02.

STERLING COUNTY, STERLING CITY. Indian fighter W. S. Sterling reached Sterling County in 1858. He hunted buffalo and marketed hides at Fort Concho in the sixties. He was killed by Apaches while serving as a United States marshal in Arizona.

Sterling County was organized in 1891 after having been cut out of Tom Green County. Two courthouses existed at Sterling City before the present $90,000 edifice was built in 1938.

STONEWALL COUNTY, ASPERMONT. In the late seventies, headquarters for buffalo hunters was Rath City, a collection of dugouts fourteen miles southeast of modern Aspermont. Because of Indian troubles soldiers from Fort Griffin occupied several dugouts there.

Stonewall County, created in 1876, commemorated Confederate General Thomas Jonathan "Stonewall" Jackson. Ranchers succeeded the buffalo hunters and settlement began in the 1880's. Rayner, a cow camp on W. E. Rayner's ranch, became the first county seat in 1888: its stone courthouse still stands. Aspermont—the townsite donor said that was Latin for rough hill—became the county seat in 1890. The present courthouse was built in 1910 and cost $56,000.

SUTTON COUNTY, SONORA. John S. Sutton, of Delaware, spent a year at West Point, then came to Texas. He was captured by the Mexicans on the Santa Fe expedition. After his release he took part in the Mier Expedition. Sutton fought Indians during the Mexican War and was killed in the Civil War battle of Val Verde.

Sutton County was Apache country. Fort Terrett, in 1852, was the first white settlement. Created from Crockett County, Sutton County was organized in 1890 with Sonora the capital. Until the railroad arrived a lane 250 feet wide and a hundred miles long connected ranchers with the railroad at Brady. The 1891 courthouse, which cost $27,706, is still used.

SWISHER COUNTY, TULIA. James Gibson Swisher, a Tennessean and veteran of the War of 1812, was at the siege of Bexar and signed the Declaration of Independence.

Swisher County was organized in 1890. Tulia, named for Tule Creek, has always been the county seat. The lowest temperature ever recorded in Texas was Tulia's 23° below zero on February 12, 1899. Near Tule Canyon occurred one of the last major battles of the Indian wars in 1874. The first courthouse was a two-story frame building. A $56,000 three-story brick was constructed in 1907, and an expansion and renovation costing $185,000 was completed in 1962.

TARRANT COUNTY, FORT WORTH. Edward H. Tarrant moved from North Carolina to Tennessee and served under Jackson at New Orleans. Tarrant joined the Texas Army in 1835. He was a Ranger, a congressman of the Republic, and in 1841 his victory at Village Creek caused the Indians to move westward and open Tarrant County to settlement.

Tarrant County was created from Navarro County and organized in 1850. Birdville, the first settlement, was the county seat. United States Army troops sent to the area in 1849 named their camp for General William J. Worth. The Fort Worth settlement numbered about a hundred when the troops withdrew in 1853. It became the county seat in 1856.

At least two courthouses preceded the present one. The first burned in 1876. A red stone building completed in 1877 served until the present courthouse was finished in 1895. The 1958 Civil Courts Building cost $2.5 million and the Criminal Courts and Jail Building, in 1963, about $3.5 million.

TAYLOR COUNTY, ABILENE. Taylor County honors the Taylor family of the old Robertson colony. It was organized in 1878 with Buffalo Gap the county seat. The Texas and Pacific Railway Company came through the county in 1880. Abilene, on the right of way, was named for the Kansas trail town. It became the county seat in 1883. The first courthouse was at Buffalo Gap. The present courthouse, the county's fourth, was built in 1914 for $150,000.

TERRELL COUNTY, SANDERSON. Alexander W. Terrell, a Virginian, graduated from the University of Missouri and practiced law in Missouri. He was a Texas district judge, a Confederate brigadier general, and a general in the army of Maximilian, Emperor of Mexico. As a Texas legislator, he sponsored laws establishing the Railroad Commission and providing for the primary system of nominating officials. Grover Cleveland appointed him minister to Turkey.

Terrell County is ranching country. It was organized in 1905 with Sanderson, a town that had developed on the Texas and New Orleans Railroad, the county seat. Judge Roy Bean ran a Sanderson saloon for awhile.

Terrell County's only courthouse was built in 1906 for $30,000 and was remodeled in 1930.

TERRY COUNTY, BROWNFIELD. Kentuckian Benjamin Franklin Terry came to Brazoria when he was ten years old. He was a Secession Convention delegate and fought at First Manassas. He raised the 8th Texas Cavalry Regiment, Terry's Texas Rangers, and was killed in action December 17, 1861.

Brownfield defeated Gomez to be the capital of Terry County in 1904. Lumber was hauled from Colorado City for the $3,800 frame structure finished in 1906. The present building was begun in 1925 and cost—with the jail—$93,000. A 1951 addition cost $229,706.

THROCKMORTON COUNTY, THROCKMORTON. William E. Throckmorton, a Virginian, practiced medicine in Tennessee, Illinois, and Arkansas before moving to Collin County, Texas, in 1841. His son, James Webb Throckmorton, also a physician, was a brigadier general during the Civil War although he had opposed secession: after the war he was governor until General Sheridan removed him as an impediment to reconstruction.

A Lieutenant Gibson built a home near the Haskell County line in 1856, at which time the nearest house west of him was in New Mexico.

Throckmorton County was created in 1858 with Williamburg the county seat. Indian troubles and the Civil War delayed organization until 1879. The original courthouse, at Throckmorton, is still in service. It cost $16,450 in 1890, when the county had only 124 residents. An annex cost $19,748 in 1938.

TITUS COUNTY, MOUNT PLEASANT. In 1839 Andrew Jackson Titus brought his family from Tennessee to Red River County. He worked for annexation, served in the Mexican War, and was a legislator.

Titus County was created from Bowie and Red River counties and organized in 1846. Mount Pleasant was founded to serve as the county seat. The 1850 census showed 3,636 residents. In the next decade the population reached 9,648. The present courthouse was erected in 1900 at a cost of $100,000 and was remodeled in 1938 and 1962.

TOM GREEN COUNTY, SAN ANGELO. Thomas Green, a Virginian and graduate of the University of Tennessee and Princeton was a private at San Jacinto and inspector general of the Somervell Expedition. He fought in the Mexican War and was killed in action as a Confederate brigadier general in 1864.

Tom Green County was sparsely populated prior to the establishment of Fort Concho in 1867. San Angelo grew up near the fort. The county was created from Bexar County in 1874 and organized the following year. Ben Ficklin, the county seat, was destroyed in 1882 by a flood in which sixty-five people drowned. San Angelo became the county capital.

Ben Ficklin's stone courthouse was dismantled, moved to San Angelo, reconstructed, and used as the high school. In 1884 a stone courthouse was erected in San Angelo which was torn down when the present $294,000 capitol was built in 1928.

TRAVIS COUNTY, AUSTIN. Travis County honors South Carolinian William Barret Travis, who came to Anahuac, in 1831, was involved in the early disturbances which culminated in the revolution, and died in the Alamo at the age of 26.

In 1839, the two communities in Travis County were Waterloo and Montopolis. Waterloo was designated as the site for the capital of the Republic and the name was changed to Austin.

The county was organized in 1840 and the first courthouse, at Fourth and Guadalupe streets, served until 1876. The next, built in 1876 at 11th and Congress, was replaced in 1930 when the present $750,000 courthouse was completed at Tenth and Guadalupe. Wings were added and the building was remodeled in the fifties. It was again expanded and remodeled in 1962.

TRINITY COUNTY, GROVETON. The Trinity River borders Trinity County on the southeast. A tribe of Indians sold their improvements to John Gallion, then moved away in 1845, a year after the first white settlers located in the county.

Trinity County was organized in 1850 and Sumpter was the county seat until 1872. Trinity was the county seat in 1873 and 1874, and then Pennington was the capital until 1883. Groveton has been the county seat since then. Three Trinity County courthouses burned. The existing structure was finished in 1914, cost $50,000, and was remodeled in 1961.

TYLER COUNTY, WOODVILLE. Tyler County was created in 1841 as the Menard District. It was re-created and named for President John Tyler in 1846. Town Bluff was the temporary county seat. In the county seat election a site on Turkey Creek was chosen and named Woodville for George T. Wood, the sponsor of the act creating the county.

Tyler County has had three courthouses. The present one built in 1891 from the proceeds of a $30,000 bond issue, was remodeled in the thirties and sixties.

UPSHUR COUNTY, GILMER. Upshur County was named for Abel Packer Upshur who was President John Tyler's secretary of state. The county was originally Caddo country. Cherokees from the southeastern United States arrived about 1820 and fifteen years later John Cotton was the first white settler. Upshur County was created from Harrison and Nacogdoches counties and organized in 1846. Gilmer was the county seat. Slaves made up a third of the 1860 population of 10,645. At first county business was handled in someone's home. A log cabin was the first courthouse, followed by another log cabin. The third courthouse was a frame building and the fourth a brick structure that was destroyed by fire. The next brick building served until 1933, when the present courthouse was built at a cost of some $180,000.

UPTON COUNTY, RANKIN. John Cunningham Upton and William Felton Upton were Tennesseans who settled in Fayette County. John Upton, a lieutenant colonel in Hood's Texas Brigade, was killed in the Second Battle of Manassas. His brother, William, also a Hood's Brigade lieutenant colonel, was in the legislature.

Upton County was created from Tom Green County and organized thirty-six years later, in 1910. Settlement began in 1880, and the population was 501 at the time of organization. Upland was the original county seat, succeeded by Rankin in 1921. The first courthouse was at Upland. The second, at Rankin, is a $30,000 building erected in 1926. Enlargement and remodeling in 1953 cost approximately $250,000.

UVALDE COUNTY, UVALDE. Captain Juan de Ugalde served in the Spanish Army in Europe and Peru, then, in 1777, was made governor of Coahuila y Texas. For the next dozen years he fought Indians, mainly Apaches. In 1790 he defeated a band of Comanches at what became known as Cañon de Ugalde. The spelling became Uvalde, and in 1850 Uvalde County was created from Bexar. It was organized in 1853, four years after the establishment of Fort Inge made settlement possible.

After an Indian raid Mrs. Joel Fenley discovered that her sister, Mrs. Sarah Kincheloe, had sustained thirteen arrow wounds. Mrs. Fenley outlived the frontier, and her great recreation became the telephone.

Uvalde has always been the county seat. The second Uvalde County courthouse was built in 1927 and cost $200,000.

VAL VERDE COUNTY, DEL RIO. The county name commemorates the Civil War battle of Val Verde. Val verde means green valley.

Val Verde County was organized in 1885. Del Rio, the county seat, grew out of the settlement San Felipe del Rio, St. Philip of the River: the founders had arrived there on St. Philip's Day. Because there was already one San Felipe, the town became simply Del Rio. The county's only courthouse was built in 1887 at a cost of $32,000.

VAN ZANDT COUNTY, CANTON. Isaac Van Zandt, of Tennessee, practiced law at Marshall and served in the Texas Congress. Sam Houston made him chargé d'affaires to the United States.

Van Zandt County was organized in 1848 with Sabine Lake the county seat. After Wood County was created from Van Zandt, Canton became the capital. The county is often called "The Free State of Van Zandt." One explanation was that when Van Zandt was created from Henderson County, the older county retained the public debt. Van Zandt, being free of debt, was "The Free . . ."

The other explanation was that the Canton *Times* publisher asked a slave owner if he intended to bring his slaves into Van Zandt County when the Civil War began. Since the slave population was small, the owner answered he would just as soon move his slaves into a free state as bring them into Van Zandt County.

The first courthouse, built in 1857, cost $6,355. The next was constructed in 1895 and the existing $140,000 courthouse was occupied in 1937.

VICTORIA COUNTY, VICTORIA. La Salle's Fort St. Louis was located in Victoria County. Almost a century and a half separated the failure of the French colony and the beginning of permanent settlement. Martin de León began his colony in 1824 and called it Nuestra Señora de Guadalupe de Jesus Victoria. Victoria was a Mexican municipality, then one of the original counties, organized in 1837. Victoria, the county seat, was an important cattle town.

The present courthouse, built in 1892 for $75,000, is the county's second.

WALKER COUNTY, HUNTSVILLE. Texans were so grateful for his introduction of the annexation resolution that they named Walker County after Mississippi Congressman Robert J. Walker; however, after Walker became a Unionist and Texas seceded, the legislature declared that Walker County commemorated Ranger Captain Samuel H. Walker. Suggestions made to Samuel Colt by Samuel Walker resulted in a new model Colt .45, the Walker Colt. Samuel Walker was killed in action during the Mexican War.

Early settlers named Huntsville for their former home, Huntsville, Alabama: it became the county seat upon organization in 1846. The first courthouse, built in 1852, burned in 1888. The second, completed in 1889 and costing $22,495, was destroyed by fire December 24, 1968. The present building cost $821,164 in 1970.

WALLER COUNTY, HEMPSTEAD. Edwin Waller, a Virginian, fought in the revolution, signed the Declaration of Independence, and was Lamar's postmaster general. After serving as Austin's first mayor, he moved to Waller County and was a delegate to the Secession Convention.

Waller County was created from Austin and Grimes counties in 1873. Hempstead—once called "Six Shooter Junction" because of an inordinate rowdiness—has always been the county seat. The first courthouse was a wooden building called the Texas House. The second was a $9,500 two-story brick structure that was built in 1876 and burned in 1892. In 1893 a $31,000 masonry courthouse was completed. The present courthouse cost $600,000 in 1955.

WARD COUNTY, MONAHANS. Thomas William Ward, a native of Ireland, lived in Quebec and Louisiana and came to Texas with the New Orleans Greys. As one of Ben Milam's volunteers he lost a leg at Bexar, but he recruited a company and served the balance of the war under General Rusk. In 1841 he lost his right arm in a cannon accident celebrating Texas independence. He was mayor of Austin, commissioner of the General Land Office, consul to Panama, and an opponent of secession.

Settlement was increased only slightly by the 1881 arrival of the Texas and Pacific Railway: after nine years the county had only 77 residents. Ward was created from Tom Green County in 1887 and organized in 1892 with Barstow the county seat. The first permanent courthouse and jail, costing $15,182, were finished in 1893. Oil activity made Monahans the most important county town, and the government was moved there in 1939. The present courthouse, Ward County's second, was occupied in 1940 and cost $250,000.

WASHINGTON COUNTY, BRENHAM. Washington-on-the-Brazos was named by a settler for his hometown, Washington, Georgia. The Austin colonists began arriving in the early twenties. Washington-on-the-Brazos had its beginnings in 1830 and the area became a Mexican municipality. In 1836 the Declaration of Independence was signed at Washington-on-the-Brazos and it was the Texas capital in 1842.

Washington County was created in 1836 with Washington-on-the-Brazos the county seat. After other counties were formed from Washington territory, Brenham became the seat of government in 1844. Three courthouses preceded the present 1939, $200,000 model.

WEBB COUNTY, LAREDO. James Webb studied law in Virginia, served in the War of 1812, and was a federal judge in Florida before he moved to Houston in 1838. He was Lamar's secretary of state and attorney general. As supreme court reporters, he and Thomas Duval produced the first three volumes of the *Texas Reports*. Later he was a district judge.

Tomás Sánchez founded Laredo in 1755, naming it for a town in Spain. Laredo citizens took no part in the Texas Revolution. A ball was given in his honor as Santa Anna passed through on his way to Bexar shortly before the Alamo fell. After San Jacinto, Laredo citizens were interested in such revolutionary movements as the Republic of the Rio Grande which, in 1840, had its headquarters there.

Webb County was organized in 1848 with Laredo the county seat. The courthouse now in use is the county's third. It was built in 1909 and cost $60,000.

WHARTON COUNTY, WHARTON. William H. and John A. Wharton grew up in Tennessee. William H. Wharton graduated from the University of Nashville, moved to Texas in 1827, and was active in events leading to the revolution. During the siege of Bexar, Stephen Austin, Branch Archer, and Wharton were sent to the United States to get help. John Wharton was Houston's adjutant at San Jacinto.

Austin colonists settled Wharton County in 1823. By 1850 it had 1,752 residents, 1,242 of them slaves. Wharton County was created in 1846. Wharton was the county seat. The first courthouse was a modest frame building begun in 1848. The commissioners argued about the quality of the work for a couple of years. Then the commissioners ordered the courthouse wrecked and a brick building erected: it was completed in 1852 and cost about $5,200. The present courthouse was completed in 1889. It and the jail cost $100,000. The courthouse was twice remodeled and enlarged.

WHEELER COUNTY, WHEELER. After practicing law in Arkansas, Royal T. Wheeler, a Vermonter, moved to Nacogdoches in 1839. He was a supreme court justice before and after annexation.

Fort Elliott was established by the army in 1875. Wheeler County was created out of Bexar and Young counties the next year. It was the first panhandle

327

county organized, in 1879. The trading post near the fort, Mobeetie—an Indian word meaning sweet water—was the county seat. Mobeetie was badly damaged by an 1898 storm, accelerating a decline caused by being bypassed by the railroad. Wheeler became the county seat in 1906, but it was more than a year before Mobeetie citizens were reconciled to the change. In 1908 Mobeetie's frame courthouse was dismantled and reassembled in Wheeler. The existing courthouse cost $80,000 in 1925.

WICHITA COUNTY, WICHITA FALLS. The Wichita River was named for Wichita Indians Spaniards found in that area. A Wichita village stood on the site of present Wichita Falls in 1841. Thirty-three years later, well after Comanches had dispossessed the Wichitas, Colonel Ranald Mackenzie and a small force fought a Comanche band at the Wichita Falls site.

Wichita County was created in 1858 and organized the same year the Fort Worth and Denver Railroad arrived, in 1882. Wichita Falls—there was a falls of five or six feet on the river—became the county seat. The second courthouse cost $225,000 in 1916 and was given a $1.3 million remodeling in the early sixties.

WILBARGER COUNTY, VERNON. Josiah Wilbarger, of Kentucky, reached Matagorda in 1827. He taught school and surveyed. In 1833 Comanches scalped and left him for dead, but he lived another dozen years. His brother, Mathias, came to Texas in 1830.

Wilbarger County, created in 1858, was not organized until 1881 because of Indians. The first settlement was at Doan's Store on Red River in 1878. Vernon, on the Fort Worth and Denver Railroad and the Western Trail, was the county seat. It was called Eagle Flats until postal officials renamed it after Washington's Mount Vernon. The second courthouse was built in 1928 for $375,000 and still serves the county.

WILLACY COUNTY, RAYMONDVILLE. Kentuckian John G. Willacy was the legislator who introduced a bill in 1911 creating a new county from Hidalgo and Cameron. The legislature named it for him.

Spaniards first surveyed Willacy County in 1790, and a grant was made in 1793. General Phil Sheridan was in the area when he made his much-quoted statement that if he owned Texas and hell he would rent out Texas and live in hell.

Sarita was the first Willacy County seat, in 1911. Ten years later Sarita became the seat of Kenedy County and Willacy's government was moved to Raymondville, which had been in Cameron County. The first courthouse, which cost about $40,000 in 1922, is still in use.

WILLIAMSON COUNTY, GEORGETOWN. Robert M. Williamson—Three-legged Willie—suffered an illness which rendered his lower right leg useless. As a result he wore at the knee a wooden peg leg: his right foot extended out behind him. He practiced law in Georgia, moved to Texas in 1826, edited newspapers, and was active in the revolutionary movement. Just before the battle of San Jacinto he was asked to say a prayer. He concluded his request for aid with "but if you can't help us, please don't help those Mexicans." He was a judge and a congressman of the Republic.

Williamson County was organized in 1848. As the commissioners appointed to locate the county seat pondered their task George Washington Glasscock rode up on a grey mule. They offered to name the capital for him if he would give the tract where they stood. He did. George's Town resolved itself into Georgetown.

The first courthouse, a two-room cabin, served from 1850 to 1855. The second, a masonry building, was begun in 1854 and demolished in 1909. The existing courthouse cost about $115,000 and was occupied in 1911.

WILSON COUNTY, FLORESVILLE. James C. Wilson, an Englishman who had attended Oxford University, came to Texas in 1837 and was in the Somervell and Mier expeditions. He escaped from his imprisonment in Mexico in 1843. He was a legislator, judge, and Methodist minister.

Settlers from Mexico, including Erasmo Seguin, established haciendas in the county in the 1830's. Wilson County was organized in 1860 and Sutherland Springs was made the county seat. William Sutherland was the first chief justice. In 1869 legislation altering Wilson County boundaries called it Cibolo County, but that change was disregarded. For years the county seat was shuttled back and forth between Sutherland Springs and Lodi. The Lodi courthouse, built in 1872, was burned in 1883. Floresville became the capital and a large frame courthouse was built. It burned in 1884 and the present $5,000 courthouse was erected. It was renovated in 1939 and 1959.

WINKLER COUNTY, KERMIT. North Carolinian Clinton M. Winkler moved to Franklin, Texas in 1840. During the Civil War, he was a lieutenant colonel in Hood's Texas Brigade. Later he was an appellate judge.

Winkler was created from Tom Green County in 1887, but lack of population did not permit organization until 1910. Kermit, named for President Theodore Roosevelt's son, was the seat of government, since it was the county's only town. Kermit Roosevelt, a World War I pilot, was killed in action.

A severe drought lasted from 1916 to 1922. County population dropped to eighty-one in 1920. Kermit had only seven school age children. All officials had moved outside the county. Winkler County had only six legal voters just before oil was discovered in November, 1926. Within four years Winkler County population was 6,784. One courthouse preceded the present one, built in 1929 for $198,000.

WISE COUNTY, DECATUR. Henry A. Wise was United States Senator from Virginia, American minister to Brazil, governor of Virginia, and a Confederate brigadier general. He had supported Texas annexation.

Sam Woody was the first settler, in 1854. Two years later Wise County was created from Cooke County and organized. There were several sites entered in the county seat election, which was to be named Taylorsville. A 60-acre site on top of a hill near the center of the county was chosen. A small building was bought and moved to the square to be the first courthouse. Taylorsville, named for President Zachary Taylor, became Decatur, for naval hero Stephen Decatur, in 1858. In 1860 a two-story frame courthouse was erected. The next courthouse burned in 1895. The present structure, completed in 1896, cost $110,000. The granite stones were shaped and polished at the quarry near Marble Falls, then shipped to Decatur to be set into place according to the numbers written on each at the quarry.

WOOD COUNTY, QUITMAN. George T. Wood fought in the battle of Horseshoe Bend and was a Georgia legislator. He was a member of the Texas Congress and the state legislature. A regimental commander in the Mexican War, Wood became Texas' second governor.

Wood County was created from Van Zandt County in 1850. The county seat, Quitman, honored John Quitman, Mississippi governor and congressman, Mexican War general, and friend of Texas annexation. The third Wood County capitol was completed in 1925 at a cost of some $125,000. In 1949 an $155,000 addition was made.

YOAKUM COUNTY, PLAINS. Texas historian Henderson Yoakum graduated from West Point, practiced law in Tennessee, and took part in several military expeditions. In 1845, he moved to Huntsville. After serving in the Mexican War Yoakum wrote his two-volume Texas history.

Yoakum County was organized in 1907 almost a third of a century after its creation. County population was only 26 in 1900. The second Plains courthouse was a two-story frame that burned in 1926. The third is still used for some county functions. The present $260,000 courthouse was completed in 1949.

YOUNG COUNTY, GRAHAM. William C. Young came from Tennessee in 1837 and was Red River County's first sheriff. He fought in the Battle of Village Creek, was a member of the 1845 convention, and was an army officer in the Mexican War. In 1862, Confederate Colonel Young was ambushed in Cooke County.

Young County was organized in 1856 with Belknap the county seat. As settlers fell back before the Indians during the Civil War, population dropped from 592 in 1860 to 139 in 1870. The county was reorganized in 1874. Graham became the capital. Apparently, the county rented space before the first courthouse was built in 1876 on the west side of the square. The second courthouse, constructed in 1884, was demolished when the present building was completed in 1932. Its cost was $297,772.

ZAPATA COUNTY, ZAPATA. Antonio Zapata was a wealthy landowner in Tamaulipas, across the Rio Grande from Zapata County. In the late 1830's, as a Mexican Army colonel, he supported the federal faction against the Centralists. In March, 1840 Centralists captured, tried, and executed him. His head was displayed at the end of a pike in the plaza of his hometown, Guerrero, Tamaulipas.

Some settlers from Mexico took up land in Zapata County in 1750. The county was created from Starr and Webb counties in 1858. The town of Zapata, originally Carrizo, dates from about 1770. In 1953 Zapata was relocated: the new Falcon Dam inundated the old town. The present courthouse, Zapata County's third, was built then for $108,000.

ZAVALA COUNTY, CRYSTAL CITY. Zavala County was named for Lorenzo de Zavala, of Yucatan. After holding minor positions in government he was imprisoned for three years because of his beliefs. In 1821 he represented Yucatan in the Spanish Cortes in Madrid. He was a member of the Mexican Senate and governor of the State of Mexico. After he was deposed by Centralist forces he toured the United States. He joined David Burnet in a Texas empresario project, then was again governor of the State of Mexico. Santa Anna made him minister to France in 1833, but he returned from Paris and joined the Texans when Santa Anna violated the Constitution of 1824. He signed the Declaration of Independence and was ad interim vice president of the Republic.

The routes of most Spanish explorers and travelers in Texas crossed the county, but permanent settlements were not made until about 1870. Zavala County was created from Uvalde and Maverick counties in 1858, but it was not organized until 1884. Batesville was the seat of government until it was succeeded by Crystal City in 1928. The first courthouse, a $7,500 masonry building, was completed in 1885. The next, at Crystal City, cost $75,000 in 1929. A 1968 bond election funded the $350,000 courthouse completed in 1970.

Bibliography

Books

Archambeau, Ernest R., editor. *Old Tascosa, 1886-1888.* Canyon, Texas: Panhandle Plains Historical Society, 1966.

Armstrong County Historical Association, editors. *A Collection of Memories.* Hereford, Texas: Pioneer Publishers, 1965.

Benton, Wilbourn E. *Texas: Its Government and Politics.* Englewood Cliffs, New Jersey: Prentice-Hall, Inc., 1966.

Carson County Historical Survey Committee, editors. *A Time to Purpose,* 2 vol. Hereford, Texas: Pioneer Publishers, 1966.

Clark, Pat B. *The History of Clarksville and Old Red River County.* Dallas: Mathis, Van Nort and Co., 1937.

Coursey, Clark. *Courthouses of Texas.* Brownwood, Texas: Banner Printing Co., 1962.

Harris, Sallie B. *Hide Town in the Texas Panhandle.* Hereford, Texas: Pioneer Publishers, Inc., 1968.

Havins, T. R. *Something About Brown.* Brownwood, Texas: Banner Printing Co., 1958.

Hodge, Floy. *A History of Fannin County.* Hereford, Texas: Pioneer Publishers, Inc., 1966.

Hunter, Lillie. *The Book of Years.* Hereford, Texas: Pioneer Book Publishers, Inc., 1969.

Knight, Oliver. *Fort Worth, Outpost on the Trinity.* Norman: University of Oklahoma Press, 1953.

McCarty, John L. *Maverick Town, The Story of Old Tascosa.* Norman: University of Oklahoma Press, 1946.

McCleskey, Clifton. *The Government and Politics of Texas.* Boston: Little, Brown and Co., 1969.

McComb, David G. *Houston, The Bayou City.* Austin: University of Texas Press, 1969.

MacCorkle, Stuart A. and Smith, Dick. *Texas Government.* New York: McGraw-Hill Book Co., 1952.

O'Keefe, Ruth Jones. *Archer County Pioneers*. Hereford, Texas: Pioneer Book Publishers, Inc., 1969.

Patterson, Bessie. *A History of Deaf Smith County*. Hereford: Pioneer Publishers, 1964.

Smith, A. Morton. *The First Hundred Years in Cooke County*. San Antonio: The Naylor Co., 1955.

Smithwick, Noah. *The Evolution of a State*. Austin: Steck-Vaughn, 1968.

Terry County Historical Survey Committee, editors. *The Early Settlers of Terry County*. Hereford, Texas: Pioneer Book Publishers, 1968.

Texas Almanac, 1970-1971. Dallas: A. H. Belo Corporation, 1969.

Walter, Ray A. *History of Limestone County*. Austin: Von Boeckmann-Jones, 1959.

Warwick, Mrs. Clyde W. *The Randall County Story*. Hereford, Texas: Pioneer Book Publishers, Inc. 1969.

Webb, Walter P., editor. *The Handbook of Texas*, 2 vol. Austin: The Texas State Historical Association, 1952.

Williams, Annie Lee. *The History of Wharton County*. Austin: Von Boeckmann-Jones Co., 1964.

Winfrey, Dorman H. *A History of Rusk County, Texas*. Waco, Texas: Texian Press, 1961.

Special Publications

Anderson County Scenic Tours. Palestine, Texas: Anderson County Chamber of Commerce.

Fiftieth Anniversary, Jim Hogg County. Hebbronville: Hebbronville Chamber of Commerce, 1963.

The Gaines County Story, 1905-1955. Seminole, Texas, 1955.

Glenn, James L. *Centennial Reminiscence*. Rockwall, Texas, 1954.

History of the First 75 Years of Castro County, Texas. Dimmitt, Texas: Castro County Diamond Jubilee, Inc., 1966.

History of Wilson County. Floresville, Texas: Wilson County Centennial Association, Inc., 1960.

Live Oak County Centennial. George West, Texas: Live Oak
  County Centennial Association, Inc., 1956.

Lockwood, Frances B. *Comanche County Courthouses.* Comanche,
  Texas: Comanche Public Library, 1969.

McKay, Mrs. Arch and Spellings, Mrs. H. A. *A History of Jefferson,
  Marion County.* Jefferson, Texas.

Texas Permian Historical Society, editor. *A History of Ward
  County, Texas.* Monahans, Texas: Monahans Junior Chamber of
  Commerce, 1962.

Magazines

Gibson, Irene L. "San Saba's Courthouse Has Fiftieth Birthday."
  Brownwood *Bulletin,* republished in *County Progress.*
  Nov., 1961.

"Home Life On Early Ranches of Southwest Texas." *The Cattleman.*
  Fort Worth, Feb., 1938.

"Nostalgia." *The Texas Freemason.* Austin, June, 1964.

Newspapers

Bonham Daily Favorite. Bonham, Texas. October 19, 1966.

Jefferson Jimplecute. Jefferson, Texas. May 2, 1968.

Lamesa Press-Reporter. Lamesa, Texas. June 26, 1969.

Pecos Enterprise. Pecos, Texas January 21, 1969.

Scurry County Times. Snyder, Texas. December 30, 1937.

Unpublished Manuscripts

Allison, T. J. "A Brief History of Longview and Gregg County."
  March 20, 1930.

Crane, Judge R. C. "History of the Post." 1955.

Jordan, Mrs. Ruby, compiler. "History of Chambers County."

Hartsell, Mrs. Horace. "Early History of Lubbock." Sept. 1953.

Pollard, Neva. "History of Jim Wells County" unpublished
  master's thesis, Texas A & I, 1945.

Richey, Ray. "History of Morris County."

Smyer, Joe Pate. "Early Days in McMullen County."

Sources

I am indebted to the following individuals for furnishing information on their respective counties.

Anderson: Judge N.R. Link, Mrs. Sam Ballard, Carl Avera, Hilda Shamburger. Andrews: Judge Roy D. Bennett. Angelina: Judge O.L. Hubbard, J.T. Maroney. Aransas: Judge John Wendell. Archer: Judge B.G. Holder. Armstrong: Judge J.E. Johnson. Atascosa: Judge David Davidson. Austin: Judge J. Lee Dittert, Jr., Betty Welsh. Bailey: Judge Glen Williams. Bandera: Judge R.H. Adams. Bastrop: Judge Jack A. Griesenbeck, Jeanne Wilkins, Mrs. W.E. Maynard. Baylor: Judge Donnell Dickson. Bee: Judge John Monroe, Ida Campbell. Bell: Judge J.F. Clawson, V. Sutton. Bexar: Archivist Richard G. Santos, Judge Charles Grace. Blanco: Judge M.B. Barrow. Borden: Judge C.C. Nunnelly. Bosque: Mrs. George H. Brooks. Brazoria: Judge Alton C. Arnold, Judge T.M. Gupton. Brazos: Judge William Vance. Brewster: Judge J.M. Brooks. Brown: Dr. T.R. Havins. Burleson: Judge Robert Gatling. Burnet: Judge Tom O'Donnell. Caldwell: Judge William D. Wilson. Calhoun: Judge Howard Hartzag. Callahan: Judge Byron R. Richardson. Cameron: Judge Oscar C. Dancy. Camp: Judge Alvin Spearman. Carson: Judge Clarence C. Williams. Cass: Judge D.H. Boon. Castro: Judge Raymond E. Wilson. Chambers: Judge O.F. Nelson, Jr. Cherokee: Judge J.W. Chandler. Childress: Judge William Black. Clay: Judge E.W. Williams. Cochran: Judge J.A. Love, Barbara Tyson. Coke: Judge W.W. Thetford. Coleman: Judge Frank Lewis. Collingsworth: Judge Zook Thomas. Colorado: Judge Willard Shuart, Judge Charles Rutta. Comal: Oscar Hass. Comanche: Judge D.F. Caraway, Mrs. Margaret Waring. Concho: Judge Carl Peek. Cooke: Judge William W. Carroll. Coryell: Judge Norman C. Storm. Cottle: Judge Roy Parks. Crane: Judge C. Bennett. Crockett: Judge Bernice Jones. Crosby: Judge Cecil Berry. Dallam: Judge W.D. Henson. Dawson: Judge Leslie C. Pratt. Deaf Smith: Judge H.C. Williams. Denton: Joella Orr. DeWitt: Judge George Trowell, Mrs. A.W. Shaffner. Dickens: Judge Martin Pope. Dimmitt: Judge Harold J. Dean. Duval: Walter Meek. Eastland: Judge Scott Bailey. Ector: Judge Gerald Fugit. Edwards: Mrs. J. Alton Miller. Ellis: Judge Milton A. Hartsfield. El Paso: Judge T.U. Moore, Donald Holmburg. Falls: Judge R.W. Hailey, Jr. Fannin: Judge Choice Moore. Fayette: Judge Henry Schovajsa. Fisher: Judge E.G. Perkins. Foard: Judge Leslie Thomas. Fort Bend: Judge Clyde Kennelly. Franklin: Judge C.H. Duvall. Freestone: Judge T.N. Evans. Frio: Judge R.D. Fitch. Gaines: Judge Chester D. Browne. Galveston: Judge Ray Holbrook. Garza: Judge J.E. Parker. Gillespie: Judge Victor H. Sagebiel. Glasscock: Judge D.W. Parker. Goliad: Judge Robert L. Person. Gonzales: Judge John A. Romberg. Gray: Judge S.R. Lenning, Jr. Grayson: Judge Les Tribble, J.C. Taliaferro. Gregg: Judge Henry Atkinson, Mrs. W.H. Alexander. Grimes: Judge H.W. Haynie. Guadalupe: Judge H.A. Glenewinkel. Hale: Judge C.L. Abernethy. Hall: Judge E. McMurry. Hamilton: Judge Herman W. Standifer, Bob Miller. Hansford: Judge Johnnie C. Lee. Hardeman: Judge Garland C. Turner. Hardin: Judge Fletcher Richardson. Harris:

Judge Madison S. Rayburn. Harrison: Judge John D. Furrh, Jr. Hartley: Judge Garland Green. Haskell: Judge B.O. Roberson, Hays: Judge Max Smith. Hemphill: Judge B.F. Conyers. Henderson: Judge Winston Reagan, Theo S. Daniel III, Judge R.H. Lee. Hidalgo: Judge J.R. Alamia. Hill: Judge J. Howard English, L.L. Wilkes. Hockley: Judge Hulon Moreland, Barbara Jester. Hopkins: Judge W.B. Kitts. Howard: Judge Lee Porter, Mrs. Floyd Mays. Hudspeth: Judge Tom Neely, Sheriff E.A. Wright. Hunt: W. Walworth Harrison. Hutchinson: Judge Norman Coffee, Nadean Spinks. Jackson: Judge L.T. Thetford. Jasper: Judge T. Gilbert Adams, Eulis Hancock. Jeff Davis: Judge Tom R. Gray. Jefferson: Judge Chester Young. Jim Hogg: Judge Homero T. Martinez, Quita Mitchell. Jim Wells: Judge T.L. Harville. Johnson: Judge Thomas E. Ball, County Auditor George L. Murphy. Jones: Judge Leon Thurman. Karnes: Judge B.A. Hartman. Kaufman: Judge Jim Markgraf. Kenedy: Judge Lee H. Lytton, Jr. Kent: Judge Bobbie Gallagher. Kerr: Judge J.R. Neuhoffer. Kimble: Judge Walter H. Leamons. King: Judge V.L. Morris. Kinney: Judge Charles Veltmann. Kleberg: Judge B.A. Brown. Lamar: Judge Lester Crutchfield. Lamb: Judge J.B. Davis. Lampasas: Judge R.L. Northington. La Salle: Judge Robert H. Coquat. Lavaca: Judge Gus J. Strauss. Lee: Judge M.F. Kieke. Liberty: Judge Thomas A. Hightower. Lipscomb: Judge E.J. Tarbox. Live Oak: Judge Harry L. Hinton. Llano: Judge R.P. McWilliams. Loving: Sheriff Elgin R. Jones. Lubbock: Judge Rodrick L. Shaw. Lynn: Judge Walter M. Mathis. McCulloch: Judge K.O. Ellington. McLennan: Judge Raymond R. Mormino. McMullen: Judge J.P. Crain. Madison: Judge J.C. Wells. Martin: Judge Jim McCoy. Mason: Judge Marcus L. Grant. Matagorda: Judge Austen H. Furse. Maverick: Judge Dan McDuff, B.E. Pingenot. Midland: Judge Barbara G. Culver. Milam: Judge Donald Humble. Mills: Judge Cecil Egger. Mitchell: Judge Bill F. Carter. Montgomery: Judge W.S. Weisinger. Moore: Judge Ezelle Fox. Morris: Judge Carlton Robison. Motley: Judge Elbert Reeves. Nacogdoches: Judge A.W. Bell, Sr. Navarro: Judge Kenneth A. Douglas. Nolan: Judge E.L. Duncan. Nueces: Judge Noah O. Kennedy, Jr. Ochiltree: Judge Clarence Morris. Oldham: Judge J.T. Singleton. Orange: Judge Charles T. Grooms. Palo Pinto: Judge John H. Smith. Panola: Judge LeRoy LaSalle. Parker: Judge Bill Ward. Parmer: Judge Archie L. Tarter. Polk: Judge Elbert Matthews. Potter: Judge W.M. Adams. Presidio: Judge W.B. Johnson. Rains: Judge Marguerite Braziel, Carolyn Potts. Randall: Judge Lloyd King. Reagan: Judge S.E. Stout, Jr. Real: Judge W.B. Sansom. Red River: Judge Gavin Watson, Jr. Reeves: Judge F.H. Ryan. Refugio: Judge T.G. Jeter. Roberts: Judge C.E. Haynes. Robertson: Judge Gervase Reagan. Rockwall: Judge Derwood Wimpee. Runnels: Judge W.H. Rampy. Rusk: Judge Paul S. Colley. San Augustine: Judge Wyatt C. Teel. San Jacinto: Judge M.N. Turley. Schleicher: Judge J.T. Ratliff. Scurry: Judge Sterling Taylor, Patricia Miller. Shackelford: Judge I.M. Chism. Shelby: Judge V.V. Pate, Mattie Dellinger. Sherman: Judge W.S. Frizzell, Jr. Smith: Morris S. Burton. Somervell: Judge Temple Summers. Starr: Judge M.J. Rodriguez, Florence Johnson Scott. Stephens: Judge Cecil Mayes. Sterling: Judge W.R. Brooks. Stonewall: Judge A.B. Barnett. Sutton: Judge J.W. Elliott, E.B. Keng. Swisher: Judge Jack L. Driskell, Mrs. F.T. Day. Tarrant: Judge Marvin B. Simpson, Jr., J.M. Williams. Taylor: Judge Roy Skaggs. Terry: Judge W.T. McKinney. Throckmorton: Judge Byrd Thorp. Tom Green: Mrs. S.F. Hignett. Travis: Judge J.H. Watson, Johnny Crow. Trinity: Judge Jewel V. Price. Tyler: Juanita Rotan. Upshur: Judge L.G. McKinley, Doyal T. Loyd. Upton: Judge Allen Moore, Billie Sue Doucette. Val Verde: Judge James

H. Lindsey. Van Zandt: Judge Robert Mayo. Walker: Judge Amos Gates. Waller: Erma V. Winfree. Ward: Judge Carl D. Estes. Washington: Judge W.O. Tomachefsky. Webb: Judge Roberto Benavides. Wharton: Judge Dorman Nickels. Wheeler: Judge G. W. Hefley. Wilbarger: Judge Henry Scott. Willacy: Judge Hubert G. Wright. Williamson: Judge Sam V. Stone. Wilson: Judge D. Richard Voges. Winkler: Judge W.E. Cook. Wise: Judge John A. Winder, Rosalie Gregg. Wood: Judge H.C. Douglas. Young: Judge Raymond Thompson, Mrs. Vernon Gracey. Zapata: Judge A.A. Flores. Zavala: Judge Irl Taylor, M. Dale Barker. Dallas: Judge W.L. Sterrett.

I am also indebted to Clark Coursey for letting me use the maps which first appeared in his *Courthouses of Texas*.

Index

Abilene, 235, 323
Adair, John, 276
Alamita, 301
Alamo, 1, 272, 275, 280, 285, 288, 289, 297, 302, 306, 324
Albany, 223, 320
Alice, 139, 300
Allred, Jimmy, 1
Alpine, 36, 275, 276
Amarillo, 6, 202, 314, 31
Anahuac, 50, 276, 279, 324
Anderson, 101, 271, 292
Anderson County, 15, 271
Anderson, Kenneth, 271
Andrews, 16, 271
Andrews County, 16, 271
Andrews, Richard, 271
Angelina County, 17, 271
Angleton, 34, 275
Anson, 141, 300
Aransas County, 18, 271, 317
Aransas River, 271
Archer City, 19, 271
Archer County, 19, 271, 272
Archer, Branch, 271, 327
Armstrong County, 6, 20, 272
Ashville, 302
Aspermont, 231, 322
Atascosa County, 21, 272
Atascosito, 305
Athens, 121, 296
Aury, Louis, 293
Austin, 1, 241, 275, 276, 292, 302, 304, 308, 324, 326
Austin, Moses, 273, 294
Austin, Stephen, 271, 272, 273, 282, 302, 304, 327
Austin County, 22, 272
Ayr, 284
Bailey County, 23, 272
Bailey, Peter, 272
Baird, 44, 277, 278
Ballinger, 214, 318
Bandera, 24, 273
Barstow, 7, 326
Bastrop, 25, 273
Bastrop, Baron de, 273
Bastrop County, 25, 273
Bat Cave, 10, 274, 299
Baxter, Will, 9
Bay City, 175, 308
Baylor County, 26, 273
Baylor, Henry, 273
Baylor University, 282
Beales, J. C., 303
Bean, Roy, 323
Beaumont, 137, 299
Beaumont, Jefferson, 299
Bee, Barnard, 273
Bee County, 27, 273
Beeville, 27, 273, 274
Bell County, 28, 274
Bell, Peter, 274
Belknap, 330
Belle Plain, 278
Bellville, 22, 272
Belton, 28, 274
Benavides, Ignacio, 300
Benavides, Jose, 300
Ben Ficklin, 324
Benjamin, 152, 303
Bettina, 319

Bexar County, 4, 5, 6, 29, 274, 276, 280, 282, 285, 291, 293, 301, 306, 309, 310, 318, 319, 322, 324, 325, 326, 327
Bevil, John, 299
Big Lake, 206, 315, 316
Big Spring, 128, 297
Black, Jacob, 288
Blanco, 274
Blanco County, 30, 274
Blanco, Victor, 274
Blue Goose, 312
Boerne, 144, 301
Boerne, Ludwig, 301
Bois d'Arc, 288
Bonham, 88, 288
Bonham, James, 288
Bonney, William, 320
Boonville, 275
Borden County, 4, 31, 274, 275
Borden, Gail, 274
Bosque, 281, 314
Bosque County, 32, 275
Boston, 33, 275
Bowie, 323
Bowie County, 4, 33, 275, 278, 280
Bowie, James, 275, 282
Brackett, Oscar, 303
Brackettville, 150, 302, 303
Bradburn, John, 298
Brady, 168, 307, 322
Brazoria, 280, 300
Brazoria County, 34, 275, 293, 318
Brazos County, 35, 275
Brazos River, 275, 280, 281, 282, 288, 289, 307
Breckenridge, 229, 321
Breckenridge, John, 321
Brenham, 253, 305, 327
Brewster County, 4, 36, 275, 276
Brewster, Henry, 275
Briscoe, Andrew, 276
Briscoe County, 37, 276
Brooks County, 38, 276
Brooks, James, 276
Brown County, 39, 276, 310
Brown, Henry, 276
Brown, Jacob, 278
Brown, John, 281
Brownfield, 237, 323
Brownsborough, 302
Brownsville, 45, 278, 300
Brownwood, 39, 276
Buchanan, 300
Buchanan County, 321
Buchanan, James, 307, 321
Buckner, 281
Bucksnort, 288
Buffalo, 296
Buffalo Gap, 323
Bullhead, 287
Bullock, Richard, 298
Burkeville, 312
Burleson County, 40, 276, 277
Burleson, Edward, 276
Burnet, 41, 277, 292, 293, 298
Burnet County, 41, 277
Burnet, David, 274, 276, 277, 296, 298, 321, 330
Bryan, 35, 275
Cabeza de Vaca, 287, 290, 312
Caddo, 4, 271, 311, 320, 324

Caldwell, 40, 276, 277, 288
Caldwell County, 42, 277
Caldwell, Mathew, 277, 284
Calhoun County, 43, 277, 316
Callahan County, 44, 277, 278
Callahan, James, 277
Calvert, 317
Cambridge, 280
Cameron, 180, 277, 285, 309, 310, 328
Cameron County, 4, 5, 45, 278, 328
Cameron, Ewen, 278
Camp Colorado, 280
Camp County, 46, 278
Camp Eagle Pass, 309
Camp Henderson, 300
Camp, Jean, 278
Campbell, Jourdan, 272
Canadian, 120, 295, 296
Canton, 248, 325
Canyon, 205, 315
Carhart, Lewis, 286
Carrizo, 330
Carrizo Springs, 78, 285
Carson City, 278
Carson County, 47, 278
Carson, Samuel, 278
Carthage, 197, 313
Cass County, 48, 278, 299
Castell, 306
Castro County, 6, 10, 49, 278, 279
Castro, Henri, 278, 309
Castroville, 278, 309
Cato, 293
Cator, Bert, 294
Cator, James, 293, 294
Cedar Springs, 284
Center, 9, 81, 224, 320
Centerville, 158, 305
Cestahowa, 301
Chambers County, 50, 279
Chambers, Thomas, 279
Channing, 117, 295
Chapin, 296
Cherokee County, 51, 279, 304
Cherokee Indians, 297, 320, 324
Chicago, 284
Childress, 52, 279
Childress County, 52, 279
Childress, George, 279
Clairemont, 302
Clarendon, 79, 286
Clark, James, 316
Clarksville, 9, 208, 285, 310, 316
Claude, 6, 20, 272
Clay County, 53, 279, 280
Cleburne, 140, 300
Cleburne, Patrick, 300
Clinton, 285
Coalson, Nick, 287
Coates, P. H., 316
Cochran County, 54, 280
Cochran, Robert, 280
Cochran, Robert, 280
Coke County, 55, 280
Coke, Richard, 280
Coldspring, 218, 318, 319
Coldwater, 320
Coleman, 46, 280
Coleman County, 56, 280
Coleman, Robert, 280
Coleman, Samuel, 315
Collin County, 57, 280

338

Collingsworth County, 10, 58, 281
Collingsworth, George, 285
Collinsworth, James, 292
Colorado City, 50, 182, 281, 310, 323
Columbus, 59, 281, 289
Comanche, 10, 61, 281, 282, 305, 306, 314
Comanche County, 9, 61, 281
Comal County, 60, 281
Comfort, 302
Concho County, 62, 282
Conroe, 184, 310, 311
Cooke County, 6, 7, 63, 279, 282, 298, 310, 329, 330
Cooke, William, 282
Coonskin, 319
Cooper, 74, 284, 285
Cooper, L. W., 284
Cora, 282
Corsicana, 189, 312
Corpus Christi, 192, 285, 302, 312, 313
Coryell County, 64, 281, 282
Coryell, James, 282
Cottle, 282
Cottle County, 65, 282
Cotton John, 325
Cotulla, 156, 304
Cotulla, Joe, 304
Cox, Paris, 283
Crane, 66, 282, 283
Crane, William, 282
Crane County, 66, 282, 283
Crockett, 127, 297
Crockett County, 67, 283, 319, 322
Crockett, David, 283, 297, 307
Crosby County, 68, 283
Crosby, Stephen, 283
Crosbyton, 68, 283
Crowell, 11, 92, 289
Crystal City, 3, 268, 330, 331
Cuero, 76, 285
Culberson, Charles, 283
Culberson County, 69, 283
Culberson, David, 283
Daingerfield, 186, 311
Dalhart, 70, 283, 284
Dallam County, 4, 70, 283
Dallam, James, 283
Dallas, 1, 5, 71, 284, 314, 320
Dallas County, 4, 11, 71, 284
Davis, 278
Davis County, 299
Davis, E. J., 280
Davis, Henry, 321
Davis, Jefferson, 299
Davis, Rancho, 321
Dawson County, 72, 284
Dawson, Nicholas, 284
De León, Alonso, 292, 309, 312
De León, Martin, 305, 326
Deaf Smith County, 73, 284
Decatur, 263, 329
Del Rio, 325
Della Plain, 289
Delta, 297
Delta County, 74, 284, 285
Denrock, 283
Denton, 75, 285
Denton County, 75, 285
Denton, John, 285
DeWitt County, 76, 285, 292
DeWitt, George, 285
DeWitt, Green, 302, 304
Dickens, 77, 285
Dickens County, 77, 285
Dickens, J., 285

Dickson, Jim, 8
Dimmitt, 49, 278, 279
Dimmitt County, 78, 285
Dimmitt, Phillip, 285
Dixie, 291
Doan's Store, 328
Dog Town, 307
Donley County, 79, 286
Donley, Stockton, 286
Dumas, 185, 311
Duval County, 80, 286
Duval, John, 286
Dyer, Walter, 315
Eagle Flats, 328
Eagle Pass, 176, 308
Eastland, 10, 81, 286
Eastland County, 81, 286
Eastland, William, 286
Ector County, 82, 286
Ector, Mathew, 286
Edinburg, 122, 296
Edwards, Benjamin, 287
Edwards County, 83, 287
Edwards, Haden, 287
Edna, 134, 299
Ellis County, 8, 84, 287
Ellis, Richard, 287
El Dorado, 221, 319
El Paso, 85, 287, 298, 303, 309, 310
El Paso County, 4, 85, 287, 298
Elkhart, 271
Emerald, 283
Emory, 204, 315
Erath County, 86, 287, 288, 307
Erath, George, 274, 275, 287, 307
Estacado, 283
Fairfield, 95, 289, 292
Falfurrias, 38, 276
Falls County, 87, 288
Fanthorp, 271
Fannin County, 8, 88, 286, 288, 292, 298, 310
Fannin, James, 288
Farwell, 199, 294, 314
Farwell, John, 314
Favor, Milton, 315
Fayette County, 89, 273, 288
Fisher County, 90, 288, 289
Fisher, Samuel, 288
Fisher, William, 321
Floresville, 261, 329
Floyd County, 91, 289
Floyd, Dolphin, 289
Floydada, 91, 289
Franklin, 212, 317
Franklin, Benjamin, 289
Franklin County, 94, 289
Fredericksburg, 100, 290
Fredonian Rebellion, 287, 314
Freestone County, 95, 289
Frio County, 96, 289
Frio Town, 290
Foard County, 11, 92, 289
Foard, Robert, 289
Fort Bend County, 93, 289
Fort Boggy, 305
Fort Brown, 278
Fort Clark, 303
Fort Concho, 321, 324
Fort Davis, 136, 299, 315
Fort Donelson, 292
Fort Elliott, 327
Fort Ewell, 304
Fort Gates, 282
Fort Griffin, 320, 322
Fort Inge, 325

Fort Leaton, 315
Fort McKavett, 309
Fort Mason, 318
Fort Mims, 283
Fort Parker, 305
Fort Ringgold, 321
Fort St. Louis, 4, 304, 326
Fort Stockton, 200, 314
Fort Terrett, 322
Fort Worth, 1, 234, 272, 285, 309, 322
Gail, 31, 274
Gaines County, 97, 290
Gaines, Edmund, 282
Gaines, James, 290
Gainesville, 7, 8, 63, 282
Gallion, John, 324
Galveston, 98, 277, 279, 290, 295, 308
Galveston County, 98, 290
Gálvez, Bernardo de, 290
Garden City, 101, 291
Garza County, 99, 290
Gatesville, 64, 282
Georgetown, 260, 291, 328, 329
Gibson, J. J. E., 8, 320
Giddings, 159, 304
Giddings, J. D., 305
Gillespie County, 100, 290, 306, 308
Gillespie, Richard, 290
Gilmer, 244, 278, 324, 325
Glasscock County, 101, 291
Glasscock, George, 291, 328
Glen Rose, 227, 321
Golconda, 313
Goldthwaite, 181, 310
Goliad, 4, 102, 277, 285, 286, 288, 291, 295, 301, 303
Goliad County, 102, 291
Gomez, 323
Gonzales, 103, 271, 282, 285, 288, 289, 291, 301, 302, 310
Gonzales County, 103, 291, 310
Gonzales, Rafael, 291
Goodnight, Charles, 272, 276, 289, 306, 313, 315
Goree, Robert, 303
Graham, 266, 330
Granberry, Hiram, 297
Granbury, 125
Grant, James, 303
Graves, Horatio, 293
Gray County, 104, 291
Gray, Peter, 291
Grayson County, 7, 8, 10, 105, 292, 316
Grayson, Peter, 292
Green, Thomas, 324
Greenville, 130, 298
Gregg County, 106, 292
Gregg, John, 292
Grenada, 284
Grimes County, 107, 271, 292, 304, 307, 326
Grimes, Jesse, 292
Groesbeck, 7, 161, 305
Groesbeeck, Abram, 305
Groveton, 242, 324
Guadalupe County, 108, 292
Guthrie, 149, 302
Gutiérrez-Magee expedition, 290, 293, 307, 312
Hale County, 109, 293
Hale, John, 293
Hall County, 110, 293
Hall, Warren, 293
Hallettsville, 157, 304
Hamilton, 111, 293
Hamilton County, 111, 282, 293

339

Hamilton, James, 293
Hamilton, Robert, 297
Hanna, Jesse, 310
Hansford County, 112, 293, 294
Hardeman, Bailey, 294
Hardeman County, 113, 294
Hardin County, 114, 294
Harris County, 4, 5, 115, 294
Harris, DeWitt, 276
Harris, John, 294
Harrisburg, 294
Harrison County, 5, 116, 292, 295, 313
Harrison, Jonas, 295
Harrison, William, 308
Hart, Weldon, 3, 277
Hartley, 283, 295
Hartley County, 117, 283, 295
Hartley, Oliver, 295
Hartley, Rufus, 295
Haskell, 118, 295
Haskell, Charles, 295
Haskell County, 118, 295, 323
Hayrick, 280
Hays County, 119, 295
Hays, Jack, 273, 295
Head of Elm, 310
Hebbron, James, 300
Hebbronville, 138, 299, 300
Helena, 301
Hemphill, 216, 318
Hemphill County, 120, 295, 296
Hemphill, John, 295
Hempstead, 326
Henderson, 7, 215, 286, 302, 305, 311, 318
Henderson County, 121, 296, 315, 325
Henderson, James, 293, 296
Henrietta, 53, 279, 280
Hereford, 10, 73, 284
Hewetson, James, 271, 316
Hidalgo, 296, 328
Hidalgo County, 122, 296
Hill County, 123, 296
Hill, George, 296
Hill, Pinckney, 273
Hillsboro, 123, 296
Hockley County, 124, 296, 297
Hockley, George, 296
Hogg, James, 299, 316
Homer, 271
Hondo, 177, 309
Hood County, 125, 297, 300
Hopkins County, 126, 297, 315
Hopkins, David, 297
Hord's Ridge, 284
Horrell, R. L., 8
Houston, 115, 275, 281, 288, 294, 296,
   300, 302, 311, 320, 327
Houston County, 127, 297
Houston, Sam, 274, 281, 293, 296, 297, 303,
   305, 314, 318, 321, 325
Howard County, 128, 297
Howard, Volney, 297
Hudspeth, Claude, 298
Hudspeth County, 129, 298
Hughes, Moses, 304
Hutchinson, Anderson, 298
Hutchinson County, 131, 298
Hunt County, 8, 130, 298, 315
Hunt, Memucan, 298
Huntsville, 326, 330
Ibarbo, Gil, 311
Indianola, 277
Irion County, 132, 298
Irion, Robert, 298
Jack County, 133, 298
Jack, Spencer, 292

Jacksboro, 133, 298
Jackson, 299, 322
Jackson County, 134
Jackson, Thomas, 322
Jasper, 135, 299
Jasper County, 135, 299
Jasper, William, 299, 312
Jayton, 146, 301
Jeff Davis County, 10, 136, 299
Jefferson, 172, 278, 308
Jefferson County, 8, 137, 299
Jefferson, Thomas, 299
Jim Hogg County, 138, 299
Jim Wells County, 139, 300
Johnson City, 274
Johnson County, 30, 140, 300
Johnson, Francis, 294
Johnson, Middleton, 300
Jones, Anson, 271, 300
Jones City, 300
Jones County, 141, 300
Jonesville, 271
Jourdanton, 21, 272
Junction, 148, 302
Karnes City, 142, 301
Karnes County, 142, 301
Karnes, Henry, 301
Kaufman, 143, 301
Kaufman County, 143, 301, 317
Kaufman, David, 301
Kendall County, 144, 274, 301
Kendall, George, 301
Kenedy County, 4, 5, 145, 301, 328
Kenedy, Mifflin, 301
Kent, Andrew, 301
Kent County, 146, 301
Kermit, 262, 329
Kerr County, 147, 302
Kerr, James, 302
Kerrville, 147, 302
Kimbell, George, 302
Kimble County, 148, 302
Kimbleville, 302
King, Alice, 300, 303
King County, 149, 302
King, John C., 302
King, Richard, 300, 301, 303
King, William P., 302
Kingsville, 151, 303
Kinney County, 150, 302, 303, 309
Kinney, Henry, 302, 312
Kleberg County, 151, 303
Kleberg, Robert, 303
Knight, Tom, 312
Knox County, 152, 303
Knox, Henry, 303
Kountze, 114, 294
La Bahía, 4, 291
Lafitte, Jean, 275
LaGrange, 89, 286, 288, 316
Lamar County, 153, 303, 315
Lamar, M. B., 5, 274, 277, 279, 292, 297, 303,
   305, 315, 321, 327
Lamartine, 307
Lamb County, 154, 303, 304
Lamb, George, 303
Lamesa, 72, 284
Lampasas, 155, 304
Lampasas County, 155, 304
Lampton, William, 315
La Plata, 284
Laredo, 254, 321, 327
La Salle, 4, 277, 289, 304, 305, 308, 326
La Salle County, 156, 304
Latham, John, 320
Lavaca, 277

Lavaca County, 4, 157, 304
Leakey, 207, 287, 316
Leakey, John, 316
Leal, Antonio, 318
Ledbetter, William, 320
Lee County, 159, 304, 305
Lee, Robert E., 280, 304, 308
Lefors, 291
Leon County, 158, 305, 307
Leona, 305
Lester, B. F., 273
Levelland, 124, 296, 297
Lexington, 288, 296
Liberty, 160, 294, 305
Liberty County, 160, 305, 314
Limestone County, 7, 161, 288, 289, 305
Linden, 48, 278
Linnville, 277
Lipscomb, 162, 305
Lipscomb, Abner, 305
Lipscomb County, 162, 305
Littlefield, 154, 303, 304
Littlefield, George, 304
Live Oak County, 163, 305
Livingston, 201, 314
Llano, 164, 306
Llano County, 164, 306
Lockhart, 42, 277
Lockhart, Byrd, 277
Lockney, 289
Lodi, 329
Lone Star, 289
Longview, 106, 292
Loving County, 4, 165, 306
Loving, Oliver, 306, 313
Lubbock, 3, 166, 306
Lubbock County, 4, 166, 306
Lubbock, Tom, 306
Lufkin, 17, 271
Lynn, W., 306
Lynn County, 167, 306, 307
Mackenzie, Ranald, 320, 328
McCulloch County, 168, 307
McCulloch, Ben, 307
McGloin, James, 305, 307, 319
McKinney, 57, 280, 281
McKinney, Collin, 280
McLennan County, 169, 307
McLennan, Neil, 307
McMullen County, 4, 170, 307
McMullen, John, 305, 307, 319
Madison, 3, 313
Madison County, 171, 307, 313
Madisonville, 3, 171, 307, 313
Madras, 316
Marble Falls, 329
Marfa, 203, 299, 315
Margaret, 294
Marienfield, 308
Marion, 271
Marion County, 172, 308
Marion, 271
Marion County, 172, 308
Marion, Francis, 299, 308, 312
Marlin, 87, 288
Marlin, John, 288
Marshall, 166, 295, 325
Martin County, 173, 308
Martin, Wylie, 308
Mason, 174, 308
Mason County, 174, 308
Matador, 187, 285, 302, 311
Matagorda, 283, 288, 308
Matagorda County, 175, 308
Mathias, 328
Maverick County, 176, 308, 309, 331

Maverick, Samuel, 308
Medina County, 177, 309
Medina, Pedro, 309
Medina River, 273, 309
Memphis, 110, 293
Menard, 178, 309
Menard County, 178, 309
Mentone, 165, 306
Meridian, 32, 275
Merriman, 286
Mertzon, 132, 298
Mesquiteville, 298
Meusebach, John, 306
Mexia, 7
Miami, 211, 317
Midland, 179, 309
Midland County, 179, 309
Mier Expedition, 278, 286, 288, 321,
    322, 329
Milam, Ben, 275, 276, 302, 309, 310, 326
Milam County, 10, 180, 277, 288, 309,
    310, 318
Mills County, 181, 310
Mills, John, 310
Mina, 273
Mitchell, Asa, 310
Mitchell County, 182, 310
Mitchell, Eli, 310
Mobeetie, 328
Monahans, 7, 252, 326, 327
Montague, 183, 310
Montague County, 183, 310
Montague, Daniel, 6, 310
Montezuma, 281
Montgomery, 310, 311
Montgomery County, 184, 292, 311, 316
Montgomery, Richard, 310
Montopolis, 324
Moore County, 185, 311
Moore, Edwin, 311
Morgan, 317
Morris County, 7, 186, 311
Morris, G. R., 273
Morton, 54, 280
Motley County, 187, 311
Mottley, Junius, 311
Mount Pleasant, 239, 289, 323
Mount Vernon, 94, 289, 303
Muleshoe, 23, 272
Munday, Seymour, 273
Murpheyville, 276
Nacogdoches, 4, 188, 282, 285, 297, 311, 313,
    320, 327
Nacogdoches County, 188, 298, 311, 315, 318,
    325
Navarro County, 189, 312, 314, 322
Navarro, José, 272, 282, 312
Navatasco, 272
New Boston, 275
New Braunfels, 60, 281
Newton, 190, 312
Newton County, 190, 312
Newton, John, 312
Nolan County, 10, 191, 312
Nolan, Philip, 312
Nueces County, 192, 312, 313
O'Reilley, James, 274
O'Tool, Jeremiah, 274
Oakland, 295
Oakville, 305, 306
Ochiltree County, 193, 313
Ochiltree, William, 313
Odessa, 82, 286
Old Boston, 275
Old Franklin, 317
Old Rip, 10

Old Runnels, 318
Old Viesca, 288
Old Warren, 8
Oldham County, 6, 194, 313
Oldham, Williamson, 313
Olton, 303, 304
Orange, 195, 313
Orange County, 195, 313
Oregon City, 273
Ozona, 67, 283
Paducah, 65, 282
Paint Rock, 62, 282
Palestine, 15, 271, 315
Palo Pinto, 196, 313
Palo Pinto County, 196, 313
Pampa, 104, 291
Panhandle, 47, 278
Panna Maria, 273
Panola County, 197, 313
Parilla, Diego, 271, 310
Paris, 153, 303
Parker County, 198, 313, 314
Parker, Cynthia Ann, 289, 305, 314
Parker, Daniel, 271
Parker, Isaac, 313
Parker, Quanah, 294
Parker, Silas, 314
Parmer County, 199, 314
Parmer, Martin, 314
Parnell, 317
Paschal County, 311
Pearl, 281
Pearsall, 96, 289, 290
Pecos, 209, 316
Pecos County, 200, 314
Perry, George, 313
Perryton, 193, 313
Petersburg, 304
Pinckneyville, 285
Piñeda, Alonso Alvarez de, 4, 278, 312
Pinhook, 303
Pitchford, 285, 302
Pittsburg, 8, 46, 278
Plains, 265, 330
Plainview, 109, 293
Pleasanton, 272
Plemmons, 298
Polk County, 101, 314
Polk, James, 314
Port Lavaca, 43, 277
Post, 99, 290
Post, Charles, 290
Potter County, 202, 314
Potter, Robert, 314
Powell, E. M., 283
Power, James, 271
Presidio, 290
Presidio County, 203, 276, 299, 315
Prideaux, R. O., 272
Princeton 289 324
Quanah, 113, 281, 294
Quitman, 264, 330
Quitman, John, 330
Quivira, 298
Rains County, 204, 297, 315
Rains, Emory, 315
Randal, Horace, 315
Randall County, 11, 205, 315
Ranger, 10, 273, 276, 277, 285, 307, 310, 322
Rankin, 245, 325
Raymondville, 259, 328
Rayner, W. E., 322
Reagan, 316
Reagan County, 206, 315, 316
Reagan, John, 315, 316
Real County, 4, 207, 316

Real, Julius, 316
Red River County, 208, 303, 314, 316,
    323, 330
Reeves County, 7, 8, 209, 316
Reeves, George, 316
Refugio, 210, 316, 317
Refugio County, 210, 316, 317
Republic of Texas, 5, 275, 277, 279, 280,
    281, 287, 288, 289, 290, 301, 308, 310,
    315, 317, 318, 322, 324, 331
Richards, Ruben, 8
Richmond, 93, 289, 303
Rio Grande City, 228, 321
Robert Lee, 55, 280
Roberts County, 211, 317
Roberts, John, 317
Roberts, Oran, 317
Robertson County, 212, 317
Robertson, Sterling C., 275, 279, 317
Roby, 90, 288, 289
Rockport, 18, 271, 317
Rocksprings, 83, 287
Rockwall, 213, 317
Rockwall County, 4, 312, 317
Romero, Casimir, 314
Ropesville, 296
Ross, L. S., 10, 289
Rowe's Land, 319
Rudolph, C. R., 6
Runnels County, 214, 318
Runnels, Hiram, 318
Rusk, 51, 279, 292, 316
Rusk County, 5, 7, 215, 318
Rusk, T. J., 296, 297, 311, 314, 318, 319
Sabine County, 216, 293, 318
San Angelo, 240, 324
San Antonio, 4, 29, 273, 274, 292, 295, 298,
    303, 307, 319
San Augustine, 217, 271, 318
San Augustine County, 217, 318
Sánchez, Tomás, 327
Sanderson, 236, 323
San Diego, 80, 286
San Elizario, 287
San Felipe, 272, 275, 325
San Jacinto, 1, 274, 275, 276, 280, 284, 286,
    287, 288, 289, 292, 301, 303, 307,
    310, 320, 321, 324, 327, 328
San Jacinto County, 218, 318, 319
San Marcos, 119, 295
San Patricio, 319
San Patricio County, 219, 319
San Saba, 220, 282, 319
San Saba County, 220, 319
Santa Anna, 278, 281, 286, 289, 290, 296,
    299, 327, 330, 331
Santa Fe County, 287
Sarita, 145, 301, 328
Schleicher County, 221, 319
Schleicher, Gustav, 319
Schreiner, Charles, 316
Schreiner, Emelie, 316
Scurry County, 10, 222, 319
Scurry, William, 319
Seguin, 108, 292
Seguin, Erasmo, 292, 329
Selma, 311
Seminole, 97, 290
Seymour, 26, 273
Shackelford County, 223, 320
Shackelford, John, 320
Shawnee, 271
Shelby County, 9, 295, 313, 310
Shelby, Isaac, 320
Shelbyville, 320
Sheridan, 323

341

Sherman, 105, 292
Sherman County, 225, 320
Sherman, Sidney, 292, 320
Sherwood, 298
Sierra Blanca, 129, 298
Silverton, 37, 276
Sinton, 219, 319
Smith County, 226, 320
Smith, Erastus "Deaf", 284
Smith, James, 320
Smithwick, Noah, 271, 273
Snyder, 222, 319
Snyder, W. H., 319
Somervell, Alexander, 321
Somervell County, 321
Sonora, 232, 322
Spearman, 112, 293
Springfield, 7, 305
Spurlock, Rob, 311
Stanton, 173, 308
Starr County, 228, 321, 330
Starr, James, 321
Stephens, Alexander, 321
Stephens County, 229, 321
Stephen, William, 288
Stephenville, 86, 287, 288
Sterling City, 230, 321
Sterling County, 230, 321
Stinnett, 131, 298
Stonewall County, 231, 322
Stratford, 225, 320
Strong, W. R., 8
Sulphur Springs, 126, 297
Sumpter, 324
Sutherland, William, 329
Sutton County, 232, 322
Sutton, John, 322
Swartwout, 314
Sweetwater, 10, 191, 312
Swisher County, 233, 322
Swisher, James, 322
Tahoka, 167, 306, 307
Tarrant County, 5, 234, 322
Tarrant, Edward, 285, 322
Tascosa, 6, 313
Taylor County, 235, 323
Taylorsville, 329
Tenaha, 295, 320
Terrell, Alexander, 323
Terrell County, 236, 323
Terry County, 237
Texana, 299
Texline, 284
Thomas, George, 308
Throckmorton, 238, 323
Throckmorton County, 238, 323
Throckmorton, James, 323
Tilden, 170, 307
Titus, Andrew, 323
Titus County, 7, 239, 289, 311, 323
Tom Green County, 240, 309, 321, 324, 325, 326, 329
Town Bluff, 324
Townsend, John, 285
Toyah, 7, 316
Travis County, 241, 324
Travis, William Barret, 276, 282, 288, 289, 298, 301, 302, 318, 324
Trinity, 311, 324
Trinity County, 242, 324
Troup, George, 303
Troy, 282
Tulia, 233, 322
Tulip, 288
Turkey Creek, 324
Turtle Bayou, 308

Twist, 283
Tyler, 226, 320
Tyler County, 243, 324
Tyler, John, 324
Ugalde, Juan de, 325
Upland, 325
Upshur, 292
Upshur, Abel, 324
Upshur County, 244, 278, 324, 325
Upton County, 245, 325
Upton, John, 325
Upton, William, 325
Uvalde, 325, 331
Uvalde County, 325
Val Verde County, 325
Vance, 287
Van Horn, 69, 283
Van Zandt County, 248, 325, 326, 330
Van Zandt, Isaac, 325
Vasquez, 295, 321
Vega, 194, 313
Vehlein, Joseph, 277
Velasco, 280
Velasco, Treaty of, 294
Vernon, 258, 328
Victoria, 249, 285, 319, 316
Victoria County, 249, 326
Village Creek, 322, 330
Waco, 169, 276, 280, 288, 307, 312
Walker County, 3, 303, 307, 326
Walker, Robert, 326
Walker, Samuel, 326
Waller County, 326
Waller, Edwin, 326
Wallisville, 279
Ward County, 7, 252, 326
Ward, Thomas, 326
Wardville, 300
Washington, 9, 10, 319
Washington County, 253, 327
Washington-on-the-Brazos, 327
Waterloo, 281, 324
Wayside, 6
Waxahachie, 9, 84, 287
Weatherford, 198, 310, 313
Weatherford, Jefferson, 314
Webb County, 254, 327
Webb, James, 327
Wellington, 58, 281
Wells, James, 300
West, George, 163, 305, 306
Wharton, 9, 11, 255, 327
Wharton County, 9, 10, 255, 327
Wharton, William, 272, 327
Wheeler, 256, 327, 328
Wheeler County, 256, 327
Wheeler, Royal, 327
Wheelock, 317
Wheelock, 317
Wheelock, Robert, 7
Wichita County, 257, 328
Wichita Falls, 257, 328
Wilbarger County, 258, 328
Wilbarger, Josiah, 328
Willacy County, 259, 328
Willacy, John, 328
Williamburg, 323
Williams, Stephen, 299
Williamson County, 260, 291, 328
Williamson, Robert, 328
Willis, 310
Wink, 306
Winkler, Clinton, 329
Winkler County, 262, 329
Wilson County, 261, 329
Wilson, James, 328

Wise County, 263, 329
Wise, Henry, 329
Woll, Adrian, 284, 293, 298, 308, 309, 321
Wood County, 265, 315, 325, 330
Wood, George, 324, 330
Woodville, 243, 324
Woody, Sam, 329
Worth, William, 322
Yoakum County, 265, 330
Yoakum, Henderson, 330
Young County, 266, 327, 330
Young, John, 296
Young, William, 330
Ysleta, 4, 287
Zapata, 267, 330
Zapata, Antonio, 330
Zavala County, 267, 268, 330, 331
Zavala, Lorenzo de, 277, 299, 330